THE 2024 EXCEL

THE 2024

EXCEL

Holler S. Brian

From Beginner to
Mastery in

72

hours

The All In One Absolute Beginner's
Comprehensive Guide to Learn All the
Functions & Formulas with Step-by-
Step Explanations.All Shortcuts to Save
Time & Simplify Your Job.

THE AUTHOR

Holler S. Brian: Your Guide to Tech Mastery

Holler S. Brian is a passionate tech professional with a knack for demystifying complex subjects.

His expertise spans a wide range of areas, from the intricacies of spreadsheet formulas to the inner workings of data manipulation tools. Brian's enthusiasm for technology is contagious, and his ability to translate technical jargon into clear, understandable language makes him a sought-after instructor.

Brian's experience equips him to tackle virtually any computer-related challenge. Whether you're a beginner navigating the world of spreadsheets or a seasoned user seeking to unlock advanced functionalities, Brian has the knowledge and know-how to guide you.

Brian's true talent lies in his ability to translate complex concepts into easily digestible information. He understands that the key to effective learning is clear communication and practical application. His teaching style is engaging, interactive, and focused on empowering learners to achieve their tech goals. Brian's dedication extends beyond simply imparting knowledge. He is passionate about fostering a love for learning and helping individuals leverage technology to reach their full potential. With his guidance and expertise, you'll be well on your way to conquering the ever-evolving world of technology.

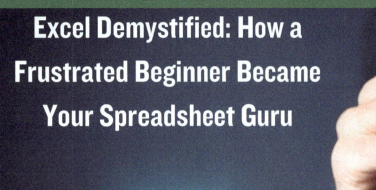

Excel Demystified: How a Frustrated Beginner Became Your Spreadsheet Guru

earnings

Confession time: spreadsheets used to terrify me. Rows, columns, formulas – it all looked like an indecipherable code reserved for tech wizards. But here's the thing: I'm Holler S. Brian, and let me tell you, Excel is not a monster lurking in your computer. It's a powerful tool waiting to be unleashed, and guess what? Anyone can learn to use it.

My journey with Excel wasn't love at first sight. It was more like staring at a foreign language textbook, feeling utterly lost. But here's the secret – we all start somewhere. My "aha" moment came when I realized Excel wasn't some mystical program, but a series of logical steps. It was like a language, and with the right approach, I could learn to speak it fluently.

Now, the beauty of Excel lies in its universality. Whether you're a student juggling budgets, a business owner managing finances, or simply someone who wants to organize their life (hello, grocery list extraordinaire!), Excel has something to offer. It's not about memorizing complex formulas (though we'll explore some handy ones!), but about understanding the core concepts and applying them to your specific needs.

Think of me as your personal translator. I've spent years deciphering the world of Excel, and I'm here to break it down into simple, actionable steps. We'll navigate the interface together, conquer those intimidating formulas (they're not so scary, I promise!), and unlock the potential to transform your data into meaningful insights. So, ditch the fear and join me on this adventure! Let's turn your Excel apprehension into spreadsheet superpowers. Together, we'll prove that Excel isn't just for the tech-savvy – it's a tool anyone can master and use to their advantage. Are you ready to unlock the magic of spreadsheets? Let's get started!

Understanding Excel Terminology

Speak the Spreadsheet Language with Confidence

Excel explorer! As you embark on your spreadsheet journey, mastering the basic vocabulary is essential. Don't worry – Excel terminology isn't complex! This book will introduce you to some fundamental terms you'll encounter frequently, equipping you to navigate the world of Excel with clarity and confidence.

The Building Blocks: Cells and Rows & Columns

Ø Cell: Imagine a spreadsheet as a giant grid. Each individual box within the grid is called a cell. A cell is the basic unit of data entry and manipulation in Excel. It can hold text, numbers, formulas, or even dates and times.

Ø Row: A row is a horizontal line of cells running across the spreadsheet. Each row is identified by a number, starting with 1 at the top and increasing sequentially as you move down.

Ø Column: A column is a vertical line of cells running down the spreadsheet. Each column is identified by a letter, starting with A on the left and progressing alphabetically as you move to the right (up to column XFD for a very large spreadsheet).

Addressing Your Data: Cell References

·Cell Reference: This is like a unique address for each cell in your spreadsheet. It's a combination of the column letter and row number (e.g., A1, B3, C10). By referencing a cell, you can use its content in formulas or calculations.

Working with Data: Numbers, Text, and Formulas

·Data: This is the information you enter into your spreadsheet. It can be numbers, text, dates, or even formulas.

·Number: Numerical values you enter into cells for calculations and data analysis. Excel recognizes different number formats, such as currency, percentages, and decimals.

·Text: Any alphanumeric characters you enter into cells, such as names, labels, or descriptions.

·Formula: A powerful tool in Excel that allows you to perform calculations automatically. Formulas begin with an equal sign (=) followed by mathematical operators, cell references, and functions.

Data Organization: Formatting and Functions

·Formatting: This refers to the way you customize the appearance of your data in cells. You can format cells to change font styles, text alignment, borders, and cell color for better readability and organization.

III

·Function: Excel has a vast library of built-in functions that perform specific tasks. For example, the SUM function adds up a range of cells, while the AVERAGE function calculates the average of a set of numbers.

Managing Your Spreadsheet: Workbooks and Worksheets

·Workbook: A workbook is like a digital binder that can hold multiple spreadsheets. Think of it as the entire file you create in Excel.

·Worksheet: Each workbook can contain one or more worksheets. A worksheet is the individual spreadsheet within a workbook, where you enter and organize your data.

Beyond the Basics: Additional Terms

As you explore Excel further, you'll encounter additional terms. Here are a few to keep in mind:

·Chart: A visual representation of your data, such as a bar graph or pie chart.

·Range: A selection of multiple cells on your worksheet.

·Sorting: Arranging data in a specific order (alphabetically, numerically, etc.).

·Filtering: Temporarily hiding certain data that doesn't meet specific criteria.

Remember: Don't be intimidated by new terminology! As you practice using Excel, these terms will become second nature. Refer back to this book as a refresher, and explore online resources or Excel help menus for additional definitions. With a bit of practice, you'll be conversing fluently in the language of spreadsheets in no time!

TABLE OF CONTENTS

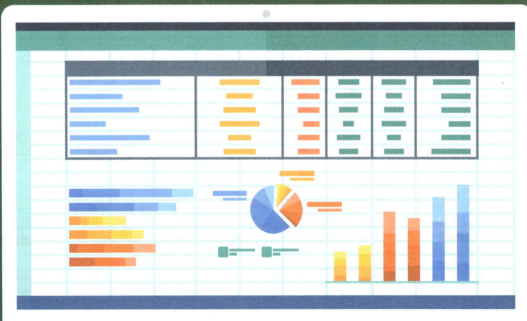

WELCOME TO EXCEL

Unveiling the Power of Spreadsheets

Congratulations on taking the first step towards mastering Excel! This powerful software is an essential tool used by millions of professionals around the world for data analysis, financial modeling, creating reports, and much more. In this book, we'll embark on a journey to unveil the exciting world of Excel and explore its capabilities.

From Humble Beginnings to Immense Potential. Spreadsheets have been a cornerstone of data management for decades. Before computers, accountants and analysts meticulously recorded information in paper ledgers with rows and columns – the very foundation of the spreadsheet concept. Fortunately, Excel takes this concept to a whole new level, transforming static data into a dynamic and interactive environment.

What Can You Achieve with Excel? Imagine a scenario where you need to track your business expenses. With Excel, you can easily create a table to record each expense, categorize it, and calculate totals. But Excel doesn't stop there! You can use formulas to automate calculations, create charts to visualize your spending patterns, and even identify areas where you can save money.

Beyond Numbers: Unveiling Hidden Gems

While Excel excels (pun intended) at numerical analysis, its capabilities extend far beyond basic calculations. You can use it to:

üManage project tasks and deadlines. Create a to-do list, set deadlines, and track progress – all within an Excel spreadsheet.

üMaintain customer databases. Organize customer information, contact details, and purchase history for easy access and analysis.

üCreate invoices and billing statements. Generate professional invoices complete with calculations and automate repetitive tasks.

üPrepare stunning presentations. Use Excel data to create charts and graphs that visually represent your findings and enhance your presentations.

The Power is in Your Hands. As you delve deeper into Excel, you'll discover a vast array of features and functions that cater to diverse needs. Whether you're a student, entrepreneur, or seasoned professional, Excel has the potential to streamline your workflow, improve your decision-making, and unlock a world of possibilities.

Ready to Begin Your Excel Adventure? This chapter provided a glimpse into the exciting world of Excel. In the following chapters, we'll delve into the specifics, guiding you through the user interface, data entry techniques, essential formulas, and powerful tools to unleash the full potential of Excel. So, buckle up and get ready to transform your data management skills!

DOWNLOADING AND INSTALLING OFFICE 2023

Your Gateway to Excel Mastery

Now that you're excited to explore the world of Excel, let's equip you with the essential tool itself – Microsoft Office 2023. This chapter will guide you through the straightforward process of downloading, installing, and activating Office 2023, ensuring you have a seamless entry point to unleashing your Excel skills.

Choosing Your Path: Free Trial or Paid Purchase

Microsoft offers two primary ways to access Office 2023:

Ø **Free Trial:** This option allows you to test drive all the features of Office 2023, including Excel, for a limited period (typically one month). It's a fantastic way to explore the software and see if it meets your needs before committing to a paid subscription.

Ø **Paid Purchase:** Microsoft offers various subscription plans for Office 2023. These plans provide full access to all the applications in the suite, including Word, Excel, PowerPoint, Outlook, and more. You can choose a monthly or annual subscription depending on your preference and budget.

Downloading Office 2023: A Smooth Journey

Once you've decided on your preferred method, follow these steps to download Office 2023:

1. **Head to the Official Source:** Visit the official Microsoft website (https://www.microsoft.com/en-us/microsoft-365). Or scan the above qr code.

2. **Explore Your Options:** Navigate through the available Office plans. If you're opting for a free trial, locate the "Try Free" button for the plan you're interested in (typically Microsoft 365 Personal or Family). For a paid subscription, choose the plan that best suits your needs and proceed to checkout.

3. **Create an Account or Sign In:** If you don't have a Microsoft account, creating one is a quick process. Alternatively, sign in using your existing Microsoft account.

4. **Follow the Download Instructions:** Once you've completed the chosen purchase method (entering payment details for paid plans or confirming the free trial), you'll receive instructions for downloading the Office installer.

Installing Office 2023: A Breeze

The downloaded file is typically an executable setup program. Double-click on the downloaded file, and the installation process will begin. Here's what to expect:

1.   **Welcome and Permissions:** The installer will welcome you and request permission to make changes to your computer. Click "Yes" to proceed.

2.   **Installation Progress:** The installer will download and install the necessary Office components. This process might take a few minutes depending on your internet speed.

3.   **Installation Complete:** Once the installation finishes, you'll be notified. Click "Close" to complete the process.

Activating Your Office 2023: Ready for Action!

Now that Office 2023 is installed, it's time to activate it:

1.   **Launch any Office Application:** Open any Office application, such as Word or Excel.

2.   **Sign In Prompt:** You'll be prompted to sign in with your Microsoft account. This is the same account you used to download or purchase Office 2023. Enter your credentials and click "Sign In."

3.   **Activation Confirmation:** If everything is configured correctly, your Office installation will be activated, and you'll be ready to start using Excel!

Troubleshooting Tips:

·Ensure you have a stable internet connection throughout the download and installation process.

·If you encounter any error messages, refer to the official Microsoft support website (https://support.microsoft.com/en-us/contactus) for troubleshooting steps. or scan this

Congratulations! You've successfully downloaded, installed, and activated Office 2023. With Excel at your fingertips, you're now equipped to embark on your journey to data mastery. The next chapters will delve into the specifics of Excel, guiding you through its user interface, data manipulation techniques, essential formulas, and powerful tools to make you an Excel whiz in no time!

MASTERING THE KEYBOARD

Excel Shortcuts for Beginners

Welcome back, aspiring Excel guru! Now that you've successfully installed and activated Office 2023, it's time to unlock the secrets to navigating Excel like a pro – keyboard shortcuts! While navigating menus can get the job done, mastering keyboard shortcuts will significantly boost your efficiency and transform you into a true "Excel Ninja."

Why Use Keyboard Shortcuts?

ü **Speed:** Switching between tasks and manipulating data becomes lightning fast with shortcuts. No more time wasted moving your mouse around the screen!

ü **Accuracy:** Using shortcuts reduces the risk of clicking the wrong button or selecting the incorrect option.

ü **Ergonomics:** Keyboard shortcuts minimize repetitive mouse movements, improving your posture and reducing strain on your hands and wrists.

ü **Workflow Enhancement:** Once you become familiar with shortcuts, your overall workflow becomes smoother and more intuitive.

Essential Shortcuts for Everyday Use:

Let's delve into some fundamental shortcuts that will become your trusty companions in your Excel adventures:

·**Movement:**

o Arrow Keys: Navigate through cells one by one (Up, Down, Left, Right).

o Home: Move to the beginning of the current row (useful for filling data across columns).

o End: Move to the end of the current row (handy for formatting entire rows).

o PgUp/PgDn: Scroll up or down one page at a time.

o Ctrl + Home: Jump to the very first cell (A1).

o Ctrl + End: Move to the last cell with data (helps you determine the used data range).

·**Selection:**

o Ctrl + A: Select all content in the worksheet (a lifesaver for quick formatting).

o Shift + Arrow Keys: Extend your selection in the desired direction (hold Shift while pressing the arrow keys).

o Ctrl + Space: Select the entire current column.

·**Editing and Formatting:**

o F2: Edit the content of the currently selected cell.

o Ctrl + C: Copy the selected cell(s) to the clipboard.

o Ctrl + V: Paste the copied content from the clipboard.

o Ctrl + X: Cut the selected cell(s) (removes the content and stores it for pasting elsewhere).

o Ctrl + Z: Undo the last action (a lifesaver when you make a mistake!).

o Ctrl + Y: Redo the last action (useful if you accidentally undo something).

o Ctrl + B: Apply bold formatting to the selected cell(s).

o Ctrl + I: Apply italics formatting to the selected cell(s).

o Ctrl + U: Apply underline formatting to the selected cell(s).

·**Formulas and Functions:**

o F4: Cycle through different absolute and relative references in a formula (a powerful tool for referencing cells across rows and columns).

o Enter: Confirms your formula or function and applies the calculation.

o Esc: Cancels out of editing a cell or formula.

Beyond the Basics: Expanding Your Shortcut Arsenal

As you become more comfortable with Excel, consider exploring additional shortcuts for specific tasks:

·**Data Entry and Manipulation:**

o Tab: Move to the next cell in the current row (great for entering data sequentially).

o Delete: Delete the selected cell content.

o Backspace: Delete one character to the left of the cursor in the cell.

o Ctrl + D: Fill the cell below with the same content as the cell above (useful for copying data patterns).

·**Formatting and Appearance:**

o Ctrl + 1: Open the Format Cells dialog box for in-depth formatting options.

o Ctrl + Shift + $ (Dollar Sign): Apply absolute cell references in a formula (fixes the cell location when copying or dragging the formula).

·**Navigation and View:**

o Ctrl + Page Up/Page Down: Switch between worksheets within the same workbook.

o F4: Repeat your last action (works for various actions like finding and replacing text).

o Ctrl + Space: Open the "Find and Replace" dialog box (useful for locating specific data within your worksheet).

Tips for Mastering Keyboard Shortcuts

·**Practice Makes Perfect:** The more you use shortcuts, the more comfortable and ingrained they become in your workflow.

·**Customize Your Shortcuts:** While the default shortcuts are great to start with, Excel allows you to customize them to your preferences. Explore the "Customize Keyboard" option within the Excel settings to personalize your experience.

·**Start Slow and Steady:** Don't overwhelm yourself – begin with a few essential shortcuts and gradually add more to your repertoire as you gain confidence.

·**Utilize Online Resources:** Several websites and tutorials offer comprehensive lists and guides to Excel shortcuts. Utilize these resources to explore advanced shortcuts and discover functionalities.

YOUR EXCEL COMMAND CENTER

Navigating the Menu Bar with Ease

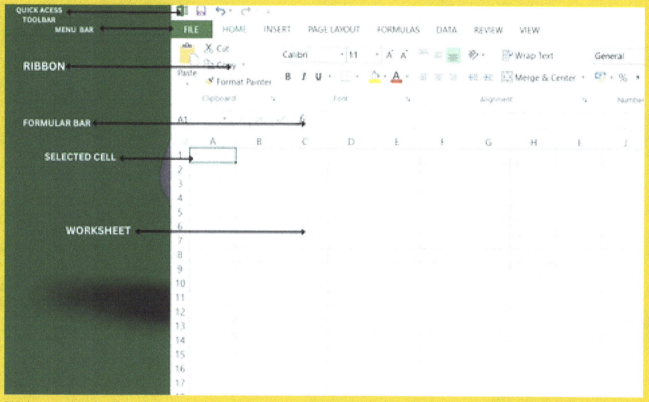

Welcome back, Excel apprentice! While the ribbon interface has become the primary command center in modern Excel versions, understanding the menu bar can still prove beneficial. This chapter will guide you through navigating the menu bar, helping you locate essential tools and functionalities within Excel.

Exploring the Menu Options:

Here's a breakdown of some key menus you'll find on the Excel menu bar:

·**File:** This menu houses options related to creating new workbooks, opening existing files, saving your work, printing worksheets, and accessing Excel settings.

·**Edit:** This menu provides tools for editing cell content, copying and pasting data, finding and replacing text, and formatting cells (although formatting options are more extensive on the ribbon).

·**View:** This menu allows you to zoom in and out on your spreadsheet, customize the ribbon's visibility, split the window for viewing different areas simultaneously, and freeze panes to keep specific rows or columns visible while scrolling.

Insert: Use this menu to insert elements into your spreadsheet, such as new rows or columns, charts, pictures, and functions.

·Format: This menu provided formatting options in previous versions, but these functionalities are now primarily found within the ribbon's "Home" and "Format Cells" tabs.

·Tools: This menu offered advanced features like spell checking, data analysis tools, and macro recording (a feature for automating repetitive tasks). While some tools are still accessible through the "Data" and "Developer" tabs on the ribbon, others have been replaced by more user-friendly functionalities.

·Window: This menu allows you to arrange multiple Excel workbooks on your screen and switch between them.

·Help: This menu provides access to Excel's help resources, tutorials, and online support.

Finding What You Need:

While the ribbon offers a more visually organized way to find commands, you can still leverage the menu bar for specific needs:

·Familiarity: If you're accustomed to the menu bar layout from older versions of Excel, you might find it quicker to access familiar tools using this method.

·Keyboard Shortcuts: Many menu options have corresponding keyboard shortcuts. By pressing "Alt" along with a specific key (often the first letter of the menu option), you can access the desired functionality without using the mouse.

The Future of the Menu Bar:

While the ribbon is the primary interface for modern Excel, the menu bar might still be present in older versions or for compatibility purposes. However, for a more efficient and user-friendly experience, it's recommended to familiarize yourself with the ribbon and its functionalities.

Remember: Don't hesitate to experiment with both the menu bar and the ribbon to discover your preferred navigation style. As you gain more experience with Excel, you'll develop your own workflow for accessing the tools you need most frequently.

Mastering the Toolbar: Your Customizable Shortcut Hub in Excel

In the ever-evolving world of Excel interfaces, the toolbar has transformed into a powerful customization tool – the Quick Access Toolbar (QAT). This chapter will equip you with the knowledge to master the QAT, turning it into your personal shortcut hub for frequently used functions and maximizing your efficiency in Excel.

From Toolbar to QAT: A Streamlined Approach

In earlier versions of Excel, toolbars displayed a collection of buttons for various functionalities. While they offered a quick way to access commands, they could become cluttered and overwhelming. The QAT streamlines this concept, allowing you to personalize which commands are readily available at your fingertips.

Locating Your QAT:

The QAT is a small toolbar positioned either above the main ribbon or below it. By default, it displays a few essential tools, but its true power lies in its customization capabilities.

Building Your Personalized Arsenal:

Here's how to transform the QAT into your personal shortcut hub:

1. **Right-click on the QAT:** This opens a context menu with various options.
2. **"Customize Quick Access Toolbar":** Select this option to open the customization window.
3. **Exploring the Treasure Trove:** You'll see a comprehensive list of commands available in Excel. From formatting options to data manipulation tools, the possibilities are vast.
4. **Picking Your Favorites:** Scroll through the list and identify commands you use frequently. Click on the desired command, then click the "Add" button. The selected command will be added to your QAT.
5. **Rearranging for Efficiency:** Once you've added your preferred commands, you can rearrange them within the QAT for optimal workflow. Simply click and hold a command, then drag it to the desired position within the toolbar.

Beyond the Basics: Advanced QAT Tips

·**Adding More Space:** If you have many frequently used commands, you can right-click on the QAT and select "Show Below the Ribbon" to create more space for your customized toolbar.

·**Resetting to Default:** If you've added too many commands and want to start fresh, right-click on the QAT and select "Reset Quick Access Toolbar."

·**Command Not Listed?** Don't worry! While the customization window displays most commands, some advanced functionalities might not be listed. You can still access them by right-clicking on the ribbon tab where they reside and selecting "Add to Quick Access Toolbar."

The Power of Personalization:

The beauty of the QAT lies in its ability to adapt to your individual needs. As you explore Excel and discover tools you use frequently, add them to your QAT to create a streamlined workspace that reflects your unique workflow. By mastering the QAT, you'll transform basic tasks into quick actions, significantly boosting your efficiency and transforming yourself into an Excel whiz!

Remember: Experimentation is key! Don't hesitate to customize your QAT, add, remove, and rearrange commands until you find a setup that optimizes your Excel experience.

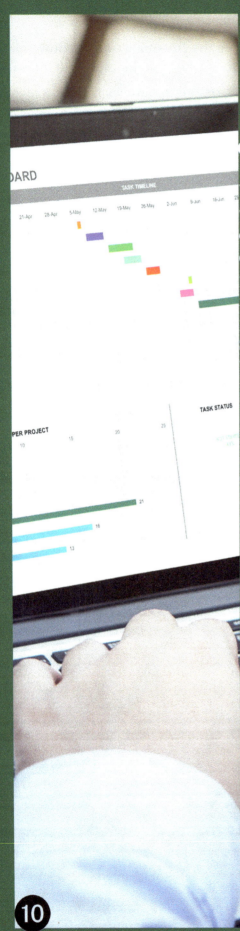

MAKE EXCEL YOUR OWN

Customizing Your Workspace for Efficiency

Welcome back, Excel adventurer! As you delve deeper into the world of spreadsheets, creating a personalized workspace is crucial for boosting your efficiency and maximizing your comfort. This chapter will guide you through a step-by-step process to customize your Excel environment, transforming it into a space that reflects your individual needs and preferences.

Step 1: Taming the Quick Access Toolbar

The Quick Access Toolbar (QAT) is a prime location for housing frequently used commands. By default, it displays some essential tools, but you can personalize it to fit your workflow.

1. **Locate the QAT:** Look for the small toolbar positioned either above the main ribbon or below it.
2. **Adding Favorite Commands:** Right-click on any empty space within the QAT. A drop-down menu will appear.
3. **Choose Your Tools:** Select "Customize Quick Access Toolbar" from the menu.
4. **Explore the Arsenal:** A window will pop up displaying a vast list of commands available in Excel.
5. **Pick Your Favorites:** Scroll through the list and locate commands you use frequently. Click on the desired command, and then click the "Add" button. The selected command will be added to your QAT.
6. **Rearranging for Ease:** Once you've added your preferred commands, you can rearrange them within the QAT for optimal workflow. Simply click and hold a command, then drag it to the desired position within the toolbar.

Step 2: Mastering the Ribbon

The ribbon houses all the essential tools and functionalities of Excel, organized into tabs. Here's how to customize it for a seamless experience:

1. **Minimizing the Ribbon:** The ribbon can be minimized for a cleaner workspace. Click the small up-arrow in the top right

corner of the ribbon to minimize it. Click the up-arrow again to expand it back to full view.

2. Customizing Tabs: You can adjust which tabs appear on the ribbon. Right-click on any tab and uncheck the box next to a tab you don't use frequently. This will hide it from the main view. To bring a hidden tab back, right-click on any visible tab, select "Customize the Ribbon," and check the box next to the desired tab.

Step 3: View Options for a Personalized Landscape

Excel offers various view options to enhance your experience:

1. Zooming In and Out: Use the zoom slider in the status bar at the bottom of your window to adjust the size of your worksheet for better viewing. You can also use keyboard shortcuts - Ctrl + Scroll Up to zoom in and Ctrl + Scroll Down to zoom out.

2. Splitting the Window: This feature allows you to work on different parts of your worksheet simultaneously. Click the "View" tab on the ribbon, then locate the "Window" section. Choose either "Split" or "Freeze Panes" depending on your preference. Split will create a horizontal or vertical dividing line, allowing you to view different sections of the worksheet. Freeze Panes allows you to freeze specific rows or columns so they remain visible while scrolling through the rest of the worksheet.

Step 4: Status Bar Tweaks

The status bar located at the bottom of the Excel window displays helpful information. Here's how to customize it:

1. **Right-click on the Status Bar:** A context menu will appear.

2. **Choose Your Information:** Select the checkboxes next to the information you want displayed in the status bar, such as Sum mode, cell coordinates, or editing mode.

Step 5: Themes – Adding a Splash of Color

Excel allows you to personalize the overall look and feel of your workspace with themes.

1. **Navigate to the "Page Layout" Tab:** Click on the "Page Layout" tab on the ribbon.

2. **Exploring Themes:** In the "Themes" section, you'll find a collection of pre-designed themes with different color schemes and styles.

3. **Choose Your Color Story:** Click on a theme to preview it on your worksheet. Once you find one that suits your preference, click on it again to apply it.

Congratulations! You've successfully customized your Excel workspace to reflect your individual needs and preferences. Remember, personalization is an ongoing process. As you continue to explore Excel, feel free to experiment with different settings and layouts to create an environment that optimizes your efficiency and makes working with spreadsheets a breeze.

THE WORKING AREA

Your Stage for Spreadsheet Mastery

Welcome back, Excel champion! Now that you're familiar with the essential tools and terminology, it's time to delve into the heart of Excel – the working area. This chapter will guide you through understanding the layout, navigating efficiently, and utilizing the working area to its full potential, transforming it into your platform for spreadsheet magic!

The Canvas of Creativity: Understanding the Layout

The working area is the central section of the Excel window where you interact with your data. It's a large grid composed of rows and columns, forming the foundation for your spreadsheets.

·**Rows:** These are horizontal lines running across the spreadsheet, identified by numbers starting with 1 at the top and increasing sequentially as you move down.

·**Columns:** These are vertical lines running down the spreadsheet, identified by letters starting with A on the left and progressing alphabetically as you move right (up to column XFD for very large spreadsheets).

The Cornerstone: Cells – Where Data Resides

Each intersection of a row and a column creates a unique cell, the fundamental building block of your spreadsheet. This is where you enter your data, be it numbers, text, formulas, or even dates and times. Cells are like tiny boxes waiting to be filled with the information that brings your spreadsheets to life.

Addressing Your Data: Cell References

Every cell has a unique address, formed by combining the column letter and row number (e.g., A1, B3, C10). This cell reference acts like a label, allowing you to pinpoint specific data within your spreadsheet. Mastering cell references is crucial for creating formulas and manipulating data effectively.

Navigating with Ease: Moving Around the Working Area

·**Arrow Keys:** Use the arrow keys on your keyboard to navigate through cells one by one (Up, Down, Left, Right).

·**Home/End Keys:** The Home key jumps you to the beginning of the current row, while End takes you to the last cell with data in that row.

·**PgUp/PgDn:** These keys scroll up or down one page at a time within the working area.

·**Ctrl + Home:** This shortcut instantly transports you to the very first cell (A1) of your worksheet.

·**Ctrl + End:** Use this shortcut to navigate to the last cell containing data in your worksheet.

Selecting Cells: Highlighting Your Data

·**Click and Drag:** Click on a cell and drag your mouse to select a range of cells.

·**Keyboard Shortcuts:** Hold down the Shift key while using the arrow keys to extend your selection in the desired direction.

·**Ctrl + A:** This shortcut selects all the content within the current worksheet, a lifesaver for quick formatting or copying entire data sets.

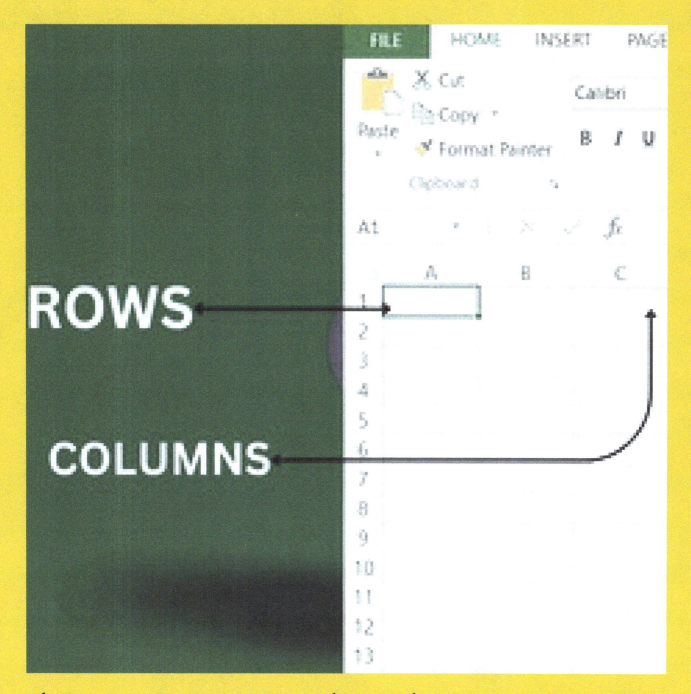

The Magic Begins: Data Entry and Manipulation

The working area is where you input your data, build formulas, and perform calculations. Here are some fundamental actions:

·**Entering Data:** Simply click on a cell and type your desired information. Excel automatically recognizes the data type (number, text, etc.) and applies basic formatting.

·**Editing Data:** To modify existing data, double-click on the cell or press F2, make your changes, and press Enter to confirm.

·**Formulas:** Unleash the power of Excel by creating formulas that perform automatic calculations. Formulas begin with an equal sign (=) followed by mathematical operators, cell references, and functions.

Mastering the Working Area: A Launchpad for Efficiency

The working area is more than just a data entry platform. Here are some additional functionalities to explore:

·**Copying and Pasting:** Use Ctrl + C to copy selected cells and Ctrl + V to paste them into another location within the worksheet or even another Excel workbook.

·**Inserting and Deleting:** Insert new rows or columns to accommodate additional data using the right-click menu within the row or column headers. You can also delete unwanted rows or columns using the same method.

·**Formatting:** Enhance the visual appeal and organization of your data by applying formatting options like font styles, borders, cell colors, and text alignment.

Remember: The working area is your command center in Excel. As you practice and explore, you'll discover its vast potential for data analysis, visualization, and creating powerful spreadsheets. By mastering the navigation, data manipulation techniques, and formatting options, you'll transform the working area into a stage for performing spreadsheet magic!

DATA ENTRY MADE EASY

AutoFill & Flash Fill – Your Excel Time-Saving Superheroes!

Welcome back, data entry warriors! Conquering spreadsheets often involves repetitive tasks like entering similar data or creating sequences. But fear not, for Excel has two built-in heroes ready to save the day – AutoFill and Flash Fill! This chapter will equip you with the knowledge to master these powerful tools, transforming your data entry experience from a chore into a breeze.

AutoFill: The Speedy Sequencer

Imagine entering a list of consecutive numbers or a series of months repeatedly. AutoFill comes to the rescue, automating the process and saving you precious time.

How AutoFill Works:

1. **Enter Your Starting Point:** Type your initial data point in a cell. For example, enter the number "1" in cell A1.

2. **Drag the Fill Handle:** Look for the small black square at the bottom right corner of the cell. This is the fill handle. Click and hold the fill handle, then drag it down (for lists) or right (for sequences) across the desired range of cells.

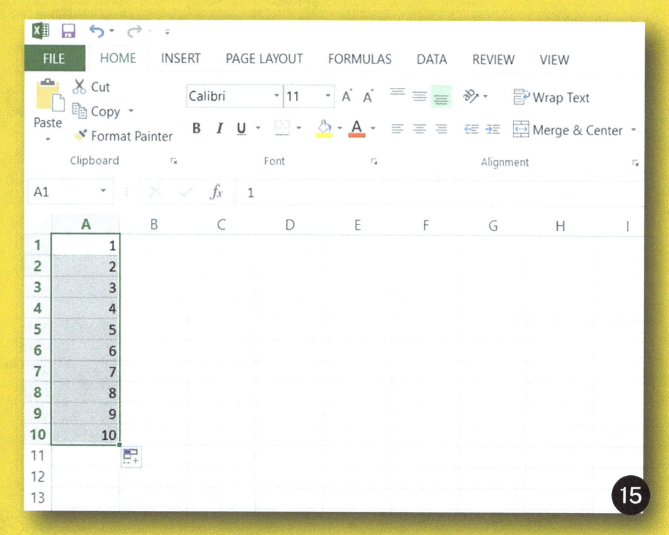

3. **Release and Watch the Magic:** As you release the fill handle, Excel automatically fills the selected cells based on the pattern it detects. In this case, it will continue the sequence by entering "2" in cell A2, "3" in A3, and so on.

AutoFill's Hidden Talents:

AutoFill isn't limited to simple sequences. It can also handle:

·**Dates:** Enter a starting date, and AutoFill will automatically fill subsequent cells with sequential dates.

·**Weekdays:** Type the first day of the week (e.g., Monday), and AutoFill will complete the remaining weekdays.

·**Series:** Create custom sequences by entering the first two or three terms of the pattern. For example, enter "1, 4, 9," and AutoFill will continue the sequence (16, 25, etc.).

Flash Fill: The Smart Data Recognizer

While AutoFill excels at patterns, what if your data entry involves filling cells with information based on existing data in your spreadsheet? Enter Flash Fill, your intelligent assistant!

Flash Fill in Action:

1. **Prepare Your Data:** Enter your sample data in a consistent format across a few rows. For example, suppose you have names in column A and corresponding email addresses (missing) in column B. John Doe's email might be "[email address removed]" in cell B2.

2. **Fill a Few Cells Manually:** In cell B3, enter the email address following the pattern you observe (e.g., "[email address removed]").

3. **Activate Flash Fill:** Select cell B3 (the cell where you entered the first manual pattern). Go to the "Data" tab on the ribbon, and locate the "Flash Fill" option in the "Data Tools" section. Click on it.

4. **Witness the Automation:** Flash Fill analyzes your existing data and the pattern you established in cell B3. It will then automatically fill the remaining cells in column B with the corresponding email addresses based on the names in column A!

Flash Fill's Superpowers:

Flash Fill isn't a one-trick pony. It can handle various data recognition tasks:

·**Extracting Text:** Separate first names from last names in a single cell.

·**Combining Text:** Create full names by merging data from separate columns.

·**Cleaning Text:** Remove unwanted characters or spaces from text entries.

Tips for Mastering AutoFill and Flash Fill:

·**Experiment:** Try using AutoFill and Flash Fill with different data sets to discover their full potential.

·**Start Small:** If you're unsure about a pattern, begin by manually filling a few cells to establish the trend for Flash Fill.

·**Clear Errors:** If Flash Fill encounters errors in your data patterns, it will highlight the problematic cells. Review your data and adjust the pattern for accurate results.

·**Practice Makes Perfect:** The more you use AutoFill and Flash Fill, the more comfortable you'l l become with their capabilities.

Embrace the Automation Revolution:

AutoFill and Flash Fill are powerful tools that can significantly reduce your data entry time and effort. By incorporating them into your workflow, you'll transform yourself from a data entry warrior into a data entry efficiency champion! Remember, Excel is packed with features designed to make your life easier. Explore these tools, experiment, and unlock the full potential of Excel's automation magic!

THE FILL SERIES TOOL

Effortlessly Create Sequential Lists

Welcome back, spreadsheet wranglers! As you navigate the exciting world of Excel, data entry often involves creating sequential lists. Numbers, dates, weekdays – the possibilities are endless. But manually typing long lists can be tedious and prone to errors. Fear not, for Excel has a dedicated tool – the Fill Series – waiting to streamline your workflow!

Unleashing the Fill Series Tool:

1. **Enter Your Starting Point:** Begin by typing the first element of your sequence into a cell. For instance, enter the number "1" in cell A1 if you want to create a list of ascending numbers.

2. **Select the Fill Range:** Click and drag your mouse to select the entire range of cells where you want the sequence to appear. Drag downwards for lists (e.g., A1:A10) or rightwards for sequences across a row (e.g., A1:B1).

Activating the Fill Series Magic:

There are two primary ways to activate the Fill Series tool:

·**Drag and Drop the Fill Handle:** Look for the small black square in the bottom right corner of the selected range. This is the fill handle. Click and hold it, then drag it downwards (for lists) or rightwards (for sequences) until you've highlighted the entire desired range. As you release the fill handle, a dropdown menu will appear.

·**Navigate Through the Ribbon:** Click on any cell within the selected range. Go to the "Home" tab on the ribbon, locate the "Editing" section, and click the dropdown arrow next to "Fill." Choose the appropriate option from the submenu (e.g., "Series," "Dates," "Weekdays").

Choosing Your Sequence Flavor:

The Fill Series dropdown menu offers a variety of options to customize your sequence:

·**Series:** This is the default option, ideal for creating sequences of numbers. Within "Series," you can further choose options like "Linear" (for ascending or descending numbers), "Growth" (for multiplying factors), or "Date" (for sequential dates).

·**Dates:** This option allows you to create sequences of dates based on a starting date and a specific interval (e.g., daily, weekly, monthly).

·**Weekdays:** Choose this option to generate a sequence of weekdays, starting from the day you entered in the first cell.

Beyond the Basics: Advanced Fill Series Techniques

The Fill Series tool offers some hidden gems for power users:

·**Custom Steps:** In the "Series" option, explore the "Step" value. By default, it's set to 1 for linear sequences. Change this value to create sequences with custom increments (e.g., enter 2 for a sequence increasing by 2s).

·**Stop Value:** Don't want your sequence to continue indefinitely? In the "Series" options, you can specify a "Stop Value" where the sequence should end.

Tips for Mastering the Fill Series Tool:

·Double-check Your Starting Point: Ensure you enter the correct starting value for your desired sequence.

·Experiment with Different Options: Explore the various "Series," "Dates," and "Weekdays" options to discover their functionalities.

·Clear Errors: If you encounter errors (e.g., insufficient space to fill the range), adjust the selected range or modify the sequence type.

Effortless List Creation:

The Fill Series tool is a valuable asset for any Excel user. By mastering this tool, you'll transform yourself from a list-typing to a list-generating champion, saving significant time and effort in your data entry endeavors. So, the next time you need to create a sequential list, remember the Fill Series tool – your secret weapon for effortless spreadsheet creation!

WORKING WITH NUMBERS

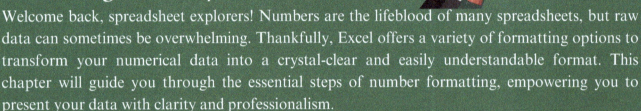

Formatting for Clarity in Excel

Welcome back, spreadsheet explorers! Numbers are the lifeblood of many spreadsheets, but raw data can sometimes be overwhelming. Thankfully, Excel offers a variety of formatting options to transform your numerical data into a crystal-clear and easily understandable format. This chapter will guide you through the essential steps of number formatting, empowering you to present your data with clarity and professionalism.

Understanding Number Formats:

Number formatting doesn't change the underlying values in your cells. It simply affects how those values are displayed visually. Excel provides a wide range of pre-designed formats to suit various data types.

Formatting Fundamentals: A Step-by-Step Guide

Let's explore how to format numbers in Excel:

1.   Select Your Numbers: Click and drag your mouse to select the cells containing the numbers you want to format.

2.   Navigate to the Home Tab: On the ribbon at the top of your Excel window, locate the "Home" tab.

3.   The Number Format Dropdown: Look for the "Number" section within the "Home" tab. You'll see a small dropdown box displaying the currently applied format (likely "General"). Click on the dropdown arrow to reveal a variety of formatting options.

4.   Choosing Your Format: Excel offers a diverse selection of number formats. Here are some commonly used options:

o   Number: This is the default format, displaying basic numbers without any decimals or commas.

o   Currency: Use this format to display numbers as currency, adding a dollar sign ($) or any other currency symbol you choose. It also automatically adds commas for better readability (e.g., $1,234.56).

o   Comma Style: This format adds commas to separate thousands, making large numbers easier to read (e.g., 1,234,567).

o   Percentage: This format displays numbers as percentages, adding a percent sign (%) after the value (e.g., 10%).

o   Decimal Places: This format allows you to specify the desired number of decimal places to be displayed (e.g., 0.00 for two decimal places).

5.Applying the Format: Once you've chosen your desired format, simply click on it in the dropdown menu. The selected format will be applied to the chosen cells.

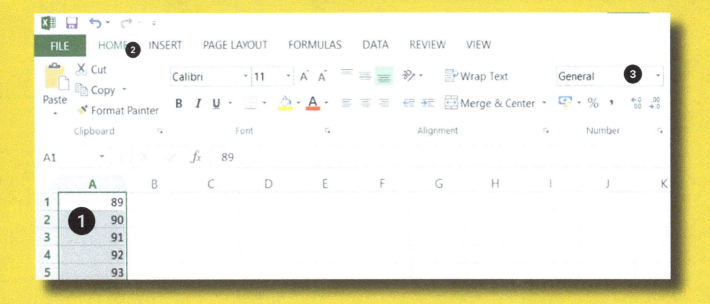

Formatting Beyond the Basics: Advanced Options

While the basic formats mentioned above cover most common scenarios, Excel offers additional formatting options to customize your data presentation:

·**Negative Numbers:** You can specify how negative numbers are displayed, such as with a minus sign (-) or parentheses around them.

·**Custom Formats:** Feeling creative? Excel allows you to create custom number formats by combining different formatting codes. This can be useful for displaying specific units or data in a particular way.

Formatting Tips for Beginners:

·**Consistency is Key:** For a professional look, strive to maintain consistent formatting throughout your spreadsheet. This improves readability and makes it easier to compare data points.

·**Clarity Reigns Supreme:** Choose a format that clearly communicates the meaning and significance of your data. For example, use currency format for financial data and percentages for representing proportions.

·**Decimal Decisions:** Don't overdo it with decimal places. Choose a number that reflects the level of precision required for your data.

The Power of Presentation:

Formatting your numbers in Excel isn't just about aesthetics; it's about effective communication. By applying appropriate formats, you can transform raw data into clear, concise, and easily interpretable information. This not only enhances the professional look of your spreadsheets but also empowers you to tell a compelling story with your numbers.

Remember: Experiment with different formats and find what works best for your specific data. With a little practice, you'll be formatting your numbers like a pro, transforming your spreadsheets into masterpieces of clarity and effective communication!

THE EXCEL TEST FUNCTION

Your Formula Debugging Superhero

Welcome back, Excel adventurers! As you venture into the exciting world of formulas, there will be times when your calculations don't yield the expected results. But fear not, for Excel has a hidden hero waiting to save the day – the TEST function! This chapter will equip you with the knowledge to wield the TEST function effectively, transforming you into a formula debugging champion.

Understanding the TEST Function:

The TEST function, often overlooked but incredibly valuable, serves a critical purpose – it allows you to evaluate the result of another formula and return either TRUE or FALSE. This functionality makes it an exceptional tool for troubleshooting and ensuring your formulas are functioning correctly.

The Anatomy of the TEST Function:

The TEST function follows a simple syntax:

Excel

=TEST(value)

•**value:** This argument represents the formula or expression you want to evaluate. It can be a direct formula you've entered into a cell or a reference to a cell containing a formula.

How the TEST Function Works:

1. **Enter the TEST Function:** In a blank cell, type the equal sign (=) to initiate a formula. Then, type "TEST" followed by an opening parenthesis.

2. **Reference Your Formula:** Inside the parentheses, enter the cell reference of the formula you want to test. Alternatively, you can directly type the formula itself within quotation marks.

3. **Close the Parenthesis:** Once you've specified the formula to be tested, close the parenthesis.

4. **Press Enter and Witness the Result:** Press the Enter key, and the TEST function will evaluate the referenced formula. It will display either TRUE (if the formula produces a valid result) or FALSE (if the formula encounters an error or returns an unexpected value).

Debugging with the TEST Function: A Step-by-Step Guide:

Let's explore how to use the TEST function to debug a formula:

1. **Identify the Suspect Formula:** If a formula isn't producing the expected outcome, suspect an error.

2. Enter the TEST Function: In a separate cell, type the TEST function, referencing the cell containing the problematic formula.

Beyond Error Checking: Additional Uses of TEST

While error checking is the primary function of TEST, it can also be used for:

·**Conditional Logic:** Combine TEST with other logical functions (AND, OR) to create complex conditional statements within your formulas.

·**Data Validation:** Use TEST to validate user input in forms. You can create a formula that checks if the entered data meets specific criteria and returns TRUE or FALSE based on the outcome.

Tips for Mastering the TEST Function:

·**Start Simple:** Begin by using TEST to evaluate basic formulas to grasp its functionality.

·Isolate the Problem: When debugging, focus on testing individual parts of your formula to pinpoint the exact source of the error.

·**Seek Help:** If you're stuck, don't hesitate to consult Excel's help resources or online communities for guidance on troubleshooting formula errors.

Your Formula Debugging Partner:

The TEST function is an invaluable tool for any Excel user who works with formulas. By incorporating it into your troubleshooting routine, you'll transform yourself from a frustrated formula fumbler into a confident formula debugger. Remember, the TEST function is always there to lend a helping hand, ensuring your formulas function flawlessly and deliver the results you expect!

DATES & TIMES UNDER CONTROL

Mastering Input and Formatting in Excel

Welcome back, spreadsheet commanders! Dates and times are essential components of many Excel workbooks. But navigating their input and formatting can sometimes feel like a challenge. Fear not, for this chapter will equip you with the knowledge to conquer dates and times in Excel, transforming you into a master of data organization and presentation!

Entering Dates and Times:

Excel offers several ways to enter dates and times:

Direct Typing: Simply type the date or time in the desired format (e.g., 2024-03-22 for a date or 10:30 AM for a time). As you type, Excel might attempt to auto-correct your entry to a recognizable date or time format.

Using Keyboard Shortcuts: Utilize keyboard shortcuts for faster data entry:

Date: Press Ctrl + D to convert the current date (displayed on your computer system) into an Excel date format.

Time: Press Ctrl + Shift + : to insert the current time.

Picking from a Calendar: Click on the small dropdown arrow in the bottom right corner of the cell. A calendar will pop up, allowing you to select the desired date visually.

Formatting Dates and Times:

Once you've entered your dates and times, it's crucial to format them for clarity and consistency:

1. Default Formatting: Excel applies a general date or time format by default. You can see the specific format by looking at the format code displayed in the number format dropdown box on the Home tab.

2. Applying Predefined Formats: Excel offers a variety of predefined date and time formats accessible through the number format dropdown menu on the Home tab. Here are some commonly used options:

Ø **Short Date:** Displays the date in a format like 3/22/2024 (US) or 22/03/2024 (UK).

Ø **Long Date:** Shows the date in a more descriptive format like Friday, March 22, 2024.

Ø **Time:** Displays the time in a format like 10:30 AM or 10:30.

Custom Formatting: Feeling creative? You can create custom date and time formats by combining different formatting codes. This allows you to display specific information like day of the week, time zone, or seconds alongside the date and time.

Formatting Tips for Effective Dates and Times:

ü **Consistency is Key:** Maintain a consistent date and time format throughout your spreadsheet for a professional look and improved readability.

ü **Clarity Reigns Supreme:** Choose a format that clearly conveys the level of detail required for your data. For example, use a format with seconds if those are crucial, but a simpler format if only hours and minutes matter.

ü **Regional Considerations:** Be mindful of regional preferences. If you're collaborating with people from different countries, consider using a format that aligns with their date and time conventions.

Beyond the Basics: Additional Considerations

ü **Serial Numbers:** Dates and times in Excel are actually stored as serial numbers. This allows Excel to perform calculations with dates and times. While you won't typically see these serial numbers, understanding their existence can be helpful for troubleshooting certain formula-related issues.

ü **Date & Time Functions:** Excel offers a vast array of functions specifically designed for working with dates and times. These functions allow you to manipulate dates, extract specific components (like day of month or year), and perform calculations involving dates and times.

Transforming Your Data:

Mastering date and time entry and formatting empowers you to organize your data effectively and present it with clarity. This not only enhances the professionalism of your spreadsheets but also allows you to analyze your data more efficiently. So, the next time you encounter dates and times in Excel, remember the techniques covered in this chapter, and watch yourself transform into a master of data organization and presentation!

DATA ENTRY ESSENTIALS

Mastering the Art of Accuracy and Efficiency

Welcome, data enthusiasts! Have you ever stumbled upon a job posting that mentions "data entry" and wondered what it entails? Well, you've landed in the perfect spot! Data entry is the foundation of countless industries, transforming physical documents, handwritten notes, or even audio recordings into digital information. This chapter equips you with the essential skills and techniques to navigate the world of data entry with confidence and efficiency.

Understanding Data Entry:

Data entry involves meticulously transferring information from various sources (paper forms, surveys, audio recordings) into a digital format, typically spreadsheets or databases. Accuracy is paramount, as errors in data entry can have far-reaching consequences. But fear not! By following these guidelines, you'll be well on your way to becoming a data entry pro.

Essential Skills for Data Entry Success:

- **Typing Skills:** Strong typing skills are the cornerstone of data entry. The ability to type accurately and efficiently minimizes errors and maximizes productivity. If you're not a touch typist (typing without looking at the keyboard), consider online typing tutorials or practice exercises to improve your speed and accuracy.
- **Attention to Detail:** A keen eye for detail is crucial. Data entry specialists must meticulously examine each piece of information and transcribe it faithfully into the digital format.
- **Data Entry Software Knowledge:** Familiarity with basic spreadsheet software like Microsoft Excel or Google Sheets is often a requirement for data entry jobs. Understanding how to navigate these applications, enter data into cells, and organize information effectively will be a valuable asset.
- **Organization and Time Management:** Data entry tasks can involve handling large volumes of information. Strong organizational skills and time management techniques will help you prioritize tasks, maintain accuracy, and meet deadlines consistently.
- **Active Listening (for Audio Data Entry):** If your data entry role involves transcribing audio recordings (like interviews or customer calls), active listening skills are essential. Pay close attention to the speaker, identify key points, and clarify any unclear information before transcribing it.

Step-by-Step Guide to Data Entry:

Let's walk through a basic data entry process:

1. **Understand the Data Entry Task:** Before starting, clearly understand the format of the source data (paper forms, digital files, audio recordings) and the desired output format (spreadsheet, database). Familiarize yourself with any specific data entry guidelines or rules provided by your employer.

2. **Prepare Your Workspace:** Ensure you have a comfortable and well-lit workspace to minimize fatigue and potential errors. Organize your source data (physical documents sorted neatly, digital files easily accessible) and have the necessary software program open and ready.

3. **Data Entry Process:** Now comes the core task! Carefully review each piece of information in the source data. Type the information accurately into the designated fields within your chosen software program (e.g., cells in a spreadsheet). Double-check your work after entering each data point to minimize errors.

4. **Data Verification:** Once you've completed data entry for a set of information, perform a thorough verification process. Proofread your work carefully, comparing the entered data to the source document. Utilize spell-checking features within your software program to catch any typos.

5. **Data Cleaning (Optional):** In some cases, the source data might contain inconsistencies or errors. Depending on your role, you might be required to clean the data before finalizing it. This could involve correcting typos, standardizing formats (e.g., date formats), or filling in missing information based on predefined rules.

Tips for Data Entry Mastery:

- **Maintain Focus:** Data entry requires sustained concentration. Take short breaks at regular intervals to avoid fatigue and maintain accuracy.
- **Utilize Keyboard Shortcuts:** Learn and utilize keyboard shortcuts in your data entry software. This can significantly boost your efficiency over time.
- **Double-Check Everything:** Develop a habit of double-checking your work regularly. This simple step can prevent errors from slipping through the cracks.
- **Ask for Clarification**: If you encounter any unclear or ambiguous information in the source data, don't hesitate to seek clarification from your supervisor or a designated team member.

Practice Makes Perfect: The more data entry experience you gain, the faster and more accurate you'll become. Practice exercises or online typing games can also help you refine your skills.

Beyond the Basics: Advanced Data Entry Techniques

As you gain experience, you might encounter more advanced data entry scenarios:

- **Batch Processing:** Here, you handle large volumes of data in groups or batches, following a specific workflow for each batch.
- **Data Validation:** Some software programs allow you to set up data validation rules. These rules automatically check if the entered data conforms to predefined criteria, minimizing the risk of errors.

- Macros and Automation: In certain data entry workflows, you might encounter repetitive tasks. Excel, for instance, allows you to create macros – small programs that automate repetitive actions. This can significantly boost your efficiency by eliminating the need to perform the same steps repeatedly. However, learning to create macros might require some additional technical knowledge.

Data Entry Tools and Technologies:

The world of data entry is constantly evolving. Here are some additional tools and technologies you might encounter:

·**Data Entry Software:** Specialized data entry software can streamline the process by offering features like pre-defined templates, data validation rules, and batch processing capabilities.

·**Data Capture Tools:** These tools can automate data entry by capturing information directly from its source (e.g., scanning barcodes on products to populate product information in a spreadsheet).

·**Optical Character Recognition (OCR):** OCR technology converts scanned images of documents (like paper forms) into editable digital text, eliminating the need for manual re-entry.

The Future of Data Entry:

Data entry is an ever-evolving field. As automation technologies like artificial intelligence (AI) advance, some data entry tasks might become automated. However, the demand for human data entry specialists with strong attention to detail and the ability to handle complex tasks will likely continue.

Data entry forms the bedrock of countless information systems. By mastering the essential skills and techniques outlined in this chapter, you'll be well-equipped to embark on a rewarding career in data entry. Remember, accuracy, efficiency, and a keen eye for detail are key to success. As you gain experience, you can explore advanced techniques, embrace new technologies, and become a valuable asset in the data-driven world!

ENSHRINING ACCURACY

Data Validation – Your Spreadsheet Guardian Angel

Welcome back, spreadsheet crusaders! Accuracy is paramount in the realm of Excel. A single erroneous entry can wreak havoc on your calculations and analyses. Fear not, for Excel offers a valiant champion in the fight for data integrity – Data Validation! This chapter equips you with the knowledge to set up data validation rules, transforming you from a data vulnerability knight into a spreadsheet accuracy champion.

Understanding Data Validation:

Data validation acts as a gatekeeper for your data, ensuring only permissible information enters specific cells. This functionality allows you to define clear rules about what type of data (numbers, text, dates) can be entered and potentially restrict the range of acceptable values.

Why Use Data Validation?

Here are some compelling reasons to leverage data validation:

·**Preventing Errors:** Human error is inevitable. Data validation acts as a safety net, preventing users from entering invalid data that could skew your results or disrupt formulas.

·**Maintaining Consistency:** Ensure consistency in your data by setting rules that limit entries to specific formats (e.g., only uppercase text, dates in a particular format).

·**Guiding Users:** Data validation can provide helpful prompts or messages to users, clarifying what type of data is expected in a cell. This can be particularly beneficial when collaborating with others on a spreadsheet.

Setting Up Data Validation Rules: A Step-by-Step Guide

Let's embark on a journey to configure data validation rules:

1. **Selecting Your Cells:** Identify the cells where you want to enforce data validation rules. Click and drag your mouse to highlight the desired range.

2. **Accessing Data Validation:** Navigate to the "Home" tab on the ribbon. Locate the "Data Tools" section and click the dropdown arrow next to "Data Validation." Alternatively, you can right-click on the selected cells and choose "Data Validation" from the context menu.

3. **The Settings Tab:** The "Data Validation" window will appear. Here, you'll define your validation rules within the "Settings" tab.

4. **Choosing the Allow Option:** Under "Allow," select the type of data you want to permit in the chosen cells. Common options include "Whole Number," "Decimal," "List," "Date," "Time," and "Text Length."

5. **Defining the Criteria:** Based on your chosen "Allow" option, further specify the criteria for valid entries within the "Data" section. Here's a breakdown of some common scenarios:

o Numbers: Set a range for acceptable values using the "Between" option. For example, you might limit a cell to accept only numbers between 1 and 100.

o List: Create a dropdown list of approved entries. Type your list items directly into the "Source" box, separated by commas.

o Dates: Specify a date range or allow only specific days (weekdays, weekends) using the "Date" options.

o Text Length: Set a minimum or maximum number of characters allowed for text entries.

6. Input Message (Optional): Provide a user-friendly message that appears when users select the cell. This message can explain what type of data is expected or offer guidance on acceptable entries.

7. Error Alert (Optional): Customize the error message displayed if users try to enter invalid data. This message can alert them to their mistake and offer corrective action.

8. Saving Your Rule: Once you've configured your desired settings, click "OK" to save the data validation rule for the selected cells.

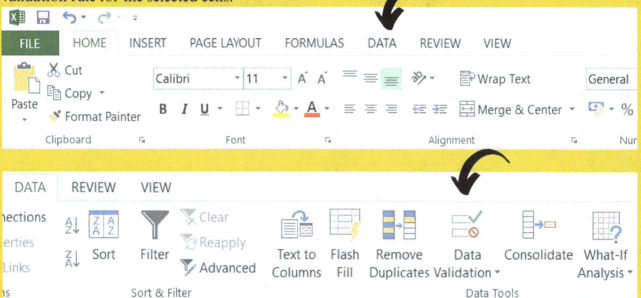

Data Validation in Action:

Imagine you're creating a spreadsheet to track product inventory. You can use data validation to:

·Restrict quantity entries to whole numbers.

·Limit product names to a specific character length.

·Create a dropdown list of available product categories.

Tips for Effective Data Validation:

·**Clarity is Key:** Ensure your data validation rules are clear and well-defined. This helps users understand what type of data is expected and avoids confusion.

·**Start Simple:** Begin with basic data validation rules for essential cells. As you gain confidence, explore more advanced options.

·**Test Thoroughly:** After setting up data validation rules, test them thoroughly to ensure they function as intended.

Your Spreadsheet Shield:

Data validation empowers you to safeguard the accuracy and integrity of your spreadsheets. By incorporating this valuable tool into your workflow, you can transform yourself from a data vulnerability knight into a champion of spreadsheet accuracy. Remember, data validation is your reliable ally in the fight for trustworthy and insightful spreadsheets!

MATH MADE EASY

Conquering Calculations with Excel

Welcome, spreadsheet novices! Numbers might seem daunting at first, but fear not! Excel acts as your friendly neighborhood math whiz, empowering you to perform basic arithmetic operations with ease. This chapter equips you with the knowledge to tackle addition, subtraction, multiplication, and division in Excel, transforming you from a math-wary user into a confident calculation champion.

Understanding Excel's Math Magic:

Excel excels (pun intended!) at numerical computations. It can handle a vast array of arithmetic operations, allowing you to analyze data, perform calculations, and generate insightful results. This chapter focuses on the fundamental building blocks: addition, subtraction, multiplication, and division.

Essentials for Performing Calculations:

Before diving into specific operations, let's explore some key things to remember:

·**Cells:** These are the building blocks of your spreadsheet, where you enter data and formulas. Each cell is identified by a unique address (e.g., A1, B2), formed by a combination of a letter (column) and a number (row).

·**Formulas:** These are instructions that tell Excel what calculations to perform. Formulas always begin with an equal sign (=) followed by the mathematical expression you want to evaluate.

·**Operators:** These symbols (+, -, , /) represent the mathematical operations you want to perform within your formula.

Performing Addition in Excel:

Adding values in Excel is a breeze! Here's a step-by-step guide:

1.   **Click on the Cell for Your Result:** Identify the cell where you want the sum to be displayed. This cell will typically be located below or to the right of the values you're adding.

2.   **Type the Equal Sign (=):** This signifies the beginning of your formula.

3.   **Enter the Cell References:** Click on the first cell containing the value you want to add. Excel will automatically display the cell address (e.g., A1) within the formula bar. You can also directly type the cell address if you know it.

4.   **Adding Operator (+):** Type the plus sign (+) to indicate addition.

5.   **Select the Second Cell (and So On):** Click on the cell containing the second value you want to add. The cell address will be appended to your formula in the formula bar, separated by the plus sign. Repeat this step for any additional values you want to include in the sum.

6.   **Press Enter:** Once you've entered all the cell references for the values you want to add, press Enter. Excel will calculate the sum and display the result in the cell you chose initially.

Let's Practice Addition:

Suppose you have sales figures in cells A1 and A2 and want to calculate the total sales in cell A3. Here's the formula you would enter in cell A3:

Excel

=A1 + A2

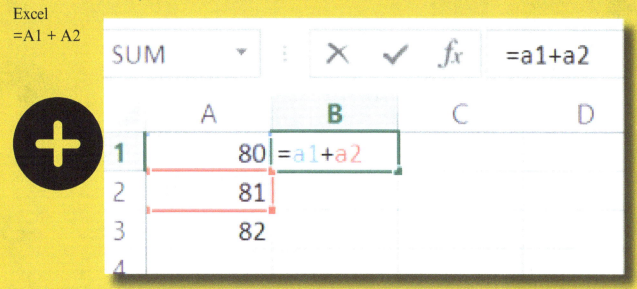

Subtracting Made Simple:

Subtracting values in Excel follows a similar logic:

1. **Choose the Result Cell:** Click on the cell where you want the difference displayed.

2. **Start with the Equal Sign (=):** This initiates your formula.

3. **Enter the First Cell Reference:** Click on the cell containing the value you're subtracting from (minuend).

4. **Subtraction Operator (-):** Type the minus sign (-) to indicate subtraction.

5. **Select the Cell to Subtract (Subtrahend):** Click on the cell containing the value you're subtracting (subtrahend). The cell address will be incorporated into your formula.

6. **Press Enter:** Hit Enter to finalize the formula. Excel will calculate the difference and display the result in your chosen cell.

Example: Profit Calculation

Imagine you have total revenue in cell B1 and expenses in cell B2. You can calculate your profit in cell B3 using the following formula:

Excel

=B1 - B2

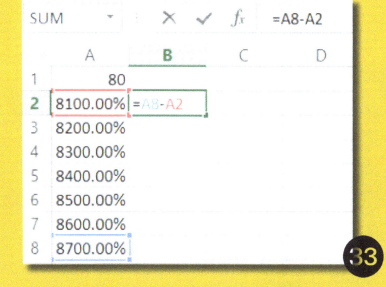

Multiplication Magic:

Multiplying values in Excel is straightforward:

1. Result Cell Selection: Click on the cell where you want the product displayed.

2. Equal Sign Initiation (=): Begin your formula with the equal sign.

3. First Cell Reference: Click on the cell containing the first value you want to multiply.

4. Multiplication Operator (): Type the asterisk () to indicate multiplication.

5. Second Cell Reference: Click on the cell containing the second value you want to multiply. The cell address will be added to your formula.

6. Press Enter: Hit Enter to complete the formula. Excel will calculate the product and display it in the chosen cell.

Division Demystified:

Dividing values in Excel is just as simple:

1. Result Cell Target: Click on the cell where you want the quotient displayed.

2. Equal Sign Introduction (=): Initiate your formula with the equal sign.

3. First Cell Reference: Click on the cell containing the value you want to divide (dividend).

4. Division Operator (/): Type the forward slash (/) to indicate division.

5. Second Cell Reference: Click on the cell containing the value you want to divide by (divisor). The cell address will be incorporated into your formula.

6. Press Enter: Hit Enter to finalize the formula. Excel will calculate the quotient and display it in the chosen cell.

Example: Average Calculation

Imagine you have exam scores in cells D1 to D5. You can calculate the average score in cell D6 using the following formula (assuming you want to include all five scores):

Excel

$$= (D1 + D2 + D3 + D4 + D5) / 5$$

Formula Tips and Tricks:

·**Cell References vs. Values:** You can directly enter numerical values within your formulas instead of using cell references. For example, =5 + 3 would calculate the sum of 5 and 3 and display the result (8) in the cell.

·**AutoSum:** Excel offers a handy AutoSum feature (located on the Home tab) that can automate some calculations. Click the AutoSum button, select the desired operation (Sum, Average, etc.), and drag your cursor over the range of cells you want to include in the calculation.

·**Order of Operations (PEMDAS):** Excel follows the order of operations (PEMDAS) when evaluating formulas. Parentheses (), Exponents ^, Multiplication and Division (/), Addition and Subtraction (+ -). Use parentheses to control the order of calculations within complex formulas.

Beyond the Basics: Exploring Additional Functions

While addition, subtraction, multiplication, and division form the foundation of calculations in Excel, the software offers a vast library of built-in functions for more complex mathematical operations. As you progress in your spreadsheet journey, you can explore functions like:

·**SUM:** Calculates the sum of a range of cells.

·**AVERAGE:** Calculates the average of a range of cells.

·**COUNT:** Counts the number of cells containing numerical values within a range.

·**COUNTIF:** Counts the number of cells within a range that meet a specific criterion.

SUM: Unveiling the Power of Addition

The SUM function, as the name suggests, calculates the sum of values within a specified range of cells. It's ideal for quickly totaling rows or columns of numerical data, saving you the time and effort of manual addition.

Using SUM: A Step-by-Step Guide

1. Click on the cell where you want the sum to be displayed. This will be the "output cell."

2. Type the SUM function followed by an opening parenthesis (.

3. Select the range of cells containing the values you want to add. You can either click and drag with your mouse to highlight the cells, or directly type the cell references (e.g., A1:A10 for cells A1 to A10).

4. Close the parenthesis).

5. Press Enter.

Example: Calculating Total Sales

Let's say you have a list of sales figures in cells B2:B10. To calculate the total sales amount, you can use the following formula:

Excel

=SUM(B2:B10)

	A	B	C	D
1	80	81	82	
2	81	91		
3	82	92	=SUM(B2:B10)	
4	83	93	SUM(**number1**, [n	
5	84	94		
6	85	95		
7	86	96		
8	87	97		
9	88	98		
10	89	99		
11	90	100		
12	91	101		

Σ

AVERAGE: Finding the Middle Ground

The AVERAGE function calculates the average (mean) of a set of numerical values within a range of cells. It's a valuable tool for understanding the central tendency of your data, providing a quick snapshot of how your data points are distributed.

Using AVERAGE: A Step-by-Step Guide

The process for using the AVERAGE function is nearly identical to SUM:

1. Click on the cell where you want the average to be displayed.

2. Type the AVERAGE function followed by an opening parenthesis (.

3. Select the range of cells containing the numerical values you want to consider for the average.

4. Close the parenthesis).

5. Press Enter.

Example: Calculating Average Test Scores

Imagine you have a list of test scores in cells C2:C15. To find the average test score, you can use the following formula:

Excel

=AVERAGE(C2:C15)

	A	B	C	D
1	80	81	82	83
2	81	91		
3	82	92	=average(b2:b10)	
4	83	93		
5	84	94		
6	85	95		
7	86	96		
8	87	97		
9	88	98		
10	89	99		
11	90	100		
12	91	101		
13	92	102		

COUNT: Taking an Inventory of Your Numbers

The COUNT function calculates the number of cells within a range that contain numerical values. It's useful for quickly determining the size of your numerical data set within a spreadsheet.

Using COUNT: A Step-by-Step Guide

1. Click on the cell where you want the count to be displayed.

2. Type the COUNT function followed by an opening parenthesis (.

3. Select the range of cells containing the data you want to count. This range can include cells with numbers, text, or even blank cells. However, only numerical values will be counted by the COUNT function.

4. Close the parenthesis).

5. Press Enter.

Example: Counting Inventory Items

Let's say you have a list of inventory items in cells A2:A20, but some cells might be blank because certain items are out of stock. To count the total number of inventory items (excluding blank cells), you can use the following formula:

Excel

=COUNT(A2:A20)

COUNTIF: Counting with Conditions

The COUNTIF function takes things a step further. It calculates the number of cells within a range that meet a specific criterion. This criterion can be a number, text, or a comparison (e.g., greater than, less than).

Using COUNTIF: A Step-by-Step Guide

1.   Click on the cell where you want the count to be displayed.

2.   Type the COUNTIF function followed by an opening parenthesis (.

3.   Select the range of cells containing the data you want to evaluate.

4.   Comma (,) After the cell range, separate it with a comma from the criteria you want to use for counting. This criteria can be:

oA number: For example, to count the number of cells in the range that contain the value 5, you would enter 5.

oText: To count the number of cells containing a specific text string (enclosed in double quotes).

oComparison operators: You can use comparison operators like `>`, `<`, `>=`, `<=`, or `<>` (not equal) to define your criteria. For example, to count the number of cells with values greater than 100, you would enter `>100`.

5. Close the parenthesis `)`.

6. Press Enter.

Example: Counting Products Above a Certain Price

Let's say you have a list of product prices in cells D2:D10. You want to count the number of products priced above $50. Here's the formula to achieve this:

```excel
=COUNTIF(D2:D10, ">50")
```

Tips for Using Math Functions Effectively:

 Understand Your Data: Ensure your data is properly formatted. Text entries or blank cells might affect the results of your calculations.

Ø **Double-Check Cell References:** Verify that you've selected the correct cell ranges for your calculations.

Ø **Nesting Functions (Optional):** You can combine these functions with other spreadsheet functions to perform more complex calculations. For instance, you could use AVERAGE within a COUNTIF formula to calculate the average value for a specific data subset.

Ø **Error Handling:** Consider incorporating error handling mechanisms (like the `IFERROR` function) to handle cases where your data might not be formatted as expected.

Beyond the Basics:

As you gain spreadsheet experience, you'll encounter a wider range of mathematical functions that can handle complex calculations, statistical analysis, and financial modeling. However, mastering the fundamentals of SUM, AVERAGE, COUNT, and COUNTIF will equip you with a solid foundation for exploring more advanced functionalities within spreadsheets.

By understanding and applying these essential math functions, you unlock the power of calculations within your spreadsheets. You can quickly analyze data, identify trends, and make informed decisions. Remember, consistent practice and exploration are key to becoming a spreadsheet whiz!

Empowering Calculations:

By mastering basic arithmetic operations in Excel, you unlock a world of possibilities for analyzing data, performing calculations, and generating valuable insights. Remember, practice is key! Experiment with different formulas, explore the AutoSum feature, and don't hesitate to consult online resources for further learning. As you gain confidence, you'll transform from a math-wary user into a spreadsheet calculation champion!

Understanding Order of Operations (PEMDAS) in Excel

Conquering calculations in Excel is not just about knowing basic arithmetic operations; it's also about understanding how Excel evaluates those operations within a formula. This understanding hinges on the concept of Order of Operations (PEMDAS).

PEMDAS serves as a mnemonic device to remember the sequence in which Excel performs calculations within a formula. It stands for:

·Parentheses

·Exponents

·Multiplication and Division (from left to right)

·Addition and Subtraction (from left to right)

Why is PEMDAS Important?

The order of operations dictates the final outcome of your formula. Performing calculations in the wrong sequence can lead to incorrect results. Here's an example to illustrate the significance of PEMDAS:

Incorrect Formula (PEMDAS Ignored):

Excel

= 6 + 3 2

Following this formula literally, Excel would perform the addition first (6 + 3) resulting in 9, and then multiply by 2, leading to a final answer of 18.

Correct Formula (PEMDAS Followed):

Excel

= (6 + 3) 2

By using parentheses, we force Excel to perform the addition within the parentheses first (6 + 3 = 9), and then multiply the result by 2, yielding the correct answer of 18.

Applying PEMDAS in Practice:

Let's explore some scenarios where understanding PEMDAS is crucial:

·**Combined Operations:** In a formula containing multiplication and addition, like =10 2 + 5, Excel will perform the multiplication first (10 2 = 20) and then add 5, resulting in 25.

·**Nested Parentheses:** Parentheses can be nested within formulas to control the order of operations even further. For example, = (2^3 + 1) 4 would calculate the exponent first (2^3 = 8), then add 1 within the parentheses (8 + 1 = 9), and finally multiply by 4, resulting in 36.

Tips for Mastering PEMDAS:

·**Break Down Complex Formulas:** If your formula involves multiple operations, consider using parentheses to explicitly define the order of calculations, especially when dealing with nested operations.

·**Use the Formula Bar Preview:** As you enter your formula, the formula bar preview in Excel displays the intermediate results based on the order of operations. This can be a helpful tool to visualize how Excel will evaluate your formula.

Understanding PEMDAS empowers you to construct accurate and reliable formulas in Excel. By following this order of operations, you can ensure that your calculations are performed in the correct sequence, leading to trustworthy results and unlocking the full potential of Excel's mathematical capabilities.

CELL REFERENCES

The Unsung Heroes of Powerful Excel Formulas

Welcome, spreadsheet voyagers! In the realm of Excel, calculations reign supreme. But what fuels these calculations? Enter cell references – the unsung heroes that empower you to weave magic with formulas. This chapter equips you with the knowledge to master cell references, transforming you from a formula fumbler into a spreadsheet calculation champion.

Understanding Cell References:

Imagine your spreadsheet as a giant chessboard. Each square, identified by a letter and a number (e.g., A1, B2, C3), is called a cell. Cell references act like coordinates, pinpointing specific cells within your spreadsheet. When you include a cell reference within a formula, you're essentially instructing Excel to fetch the value from that particular cell and use it in the calculation.

Why Use Cell References?

Cell references offer a multitude of benefits:

·**Dynamic Formulas:** By referencing other cells, your formulas automatically update when the values in those cells change. This eliminates the need to rewrite formulas for every data modification, saving you time and effort.

·**Reduced Errors:** Cell references minimize the risk of typos, as you're not directly entering values within the formula. This ensures greater accuracy in your calculations.

·**Flexibility and Power:** Cell references unlock the true potential of formulas. You can reference multiple cells across your spreadsheet, enabling complex calculations and data analysis.

Learning Cell Reference Syntax:

Cell references consist of two parts:

·**Column Letter:** Represented by a capital letter (A, B, C, and so on).

·**Row Number:** Indicated by a number (1, 2, 3, and so on).

For example, the cell reference "B3" refers to the cell located in column B and row 3 of your spreadsheet.

Referencing Another Cell – A Step-by-Step Guide:

Let's embark on a journey to create a formula that utilizes cell references:

1. **Choose the Result Cell:** Click on the cell where you want the calculated outcome to be displayed.

2. **Start with the Equal Sign (=):** This signifies the beginning of your formula.

3. **Referencing Another Cell:** Click on the cell containing the value you want to use in your calculation. Excel will automatically display the cell address (e.g., A1) within the formula bar.

4. **Operators and Additional References (Optional):** You can include mathematical operators (+, -, , /) and reference other cells within your formula to perform complex calculations.

5. **Press Enter:** Once you've constructed your formula, hit Enter. Excel will calculate the result based on the values in the referenced cells and display it in the chosen cell.

Example: Calculating Total Sales

Imagine you have sales figures in cells B2, B3, and B4. To calculate the total sales in cell B5, you can use the following formula:

Excel

=B2 + B3 + B4

In this formula, B2, B3, and B4 are cell references that instruct Excel to retrieve the values from those specific cells and add them together.

Types of Cell References:

As you delve deeper into Excel, you'll encounter various types of cell references:

·**Relative References (Default):** These references are dynamic. When you copy a formula containing a relative reference to another cell, the reference automatically adjusts based on its new position. For example, copying the formula =B2 + B3 down to cell B6 would change the reference to =C2 + C3.

·**Absolute References:** These references remain constant even when copied. You can create an absolute reference by pressing F4 while the cell reference is highlighted in the formula bar. An absolute reference includes a dollar sign ($) before the column letter and/or row number (e.g., B2).

Tips for Mastering Cell References:

·**Descriptive Cell Names:** Consider assigning meaningful names to your cells (found on the Home tab under "Define Name"). This makes your formulas easier to understand and maintain.

·**Formula Bar Preview:** The formula bar displays a live preview of your formula as you type. This helps you visualize how cell references are incorporated and identify any potential errors.

·**Practice Makes Perfect:** Experiment with different cell references in your formulas. The more you practice, the more comfortable and confident you'll become in referencing cells across your spreadsheet.

Cell References: The Powerhouse of Formulas:

By mastering cell references, you unlock the true power of formulas in Excel. You can create dynamic calculations, analyze data efficiently, and transform your spreadsheets into powerful tools for decision-making.

Utilizing Relative and Absolute References Effectively:

Understanding the distinction between relative and absolute references is crucial for building robust formulas:

·**Relative References – Champions of Flexibility:** These are the default type of reference. When you copy a formula containing a relative reference, the references automatically adjust based on their new location. This is ideal for replicating calculations across rows or columns with similar data patterns.

Example:

Imagine you have product prices in cells B2, B3, and B4, and quantities in cells C2, C3, and C4. You want to calculate the total cost for each product (price multiplied by quantity) in cells D2, D3, and D4. You can use the following formula in cell D2 and then copy it down to D3 and D4:

Excel

=B2 C2

When you copy this formula to cell D3, the relative references automatically adjust to =B3 C3, calculating the cost for the second product.

·**Absolute References – Anchoring Specificity:** Absolute references remain unchanged when copied. This is useful when you want to reference a specific cell throughout your formula, regardless of its position in the spreadsheet. You can create an absolute reference by pressing F4 while the cell reference is highlighted in the formula bar. An absolute reference includes a dollar sign ($) before the column letter and/or row number (e.g., B2).

Example:

Let's say you have a fixed tax rate of 7.5% in cell B1 (absolute reference: B1) and product costs in cells D2, D3, and D4. You want to calculate the total price including tax for each product. Here's the formula you can use in cell E2 and copy down:

Excel

=D2 (1 + B1)

In this formula, the reference to the tax rate cell (B1) is absolute, ensuring that the same tax rate is applied to all products regardless of where you copy the formula.

Combining Relative and Absolute References:

You can also combine relative and absolute references within a single formula to achieve specific calculations. For example, imagine you have a table with product names in column A, prices in column B, and you want to calculate a running total of the prices in a separate column (say, column E). Here's how you can achieve this:

Excel

=B2 + E1 (Assuming formula is placed in cell E2)

In this formula, the reference to the current price cell (B2) is relative, as you want to add the price in the cell below (B3) when you copy the formula down. However, the reference to the running total (E1) is absolute. This ensures that the formula always sums the current price with the total from the previous row, regardless of its copied position.

Advanced Cell Referencing Techniques:

As you progress in your Excel journey, you'll encounter more advanced cell referencing techniques:

·**Range References:** These references encompass a group of cells (e.g., A1:A10) instead of a single cell. You can use range references in formulas that involve calculations on multiple values within a range.

·**Indirect References:** These references allow you to use the value stored in one cell as the cell address for another cell. This can be helpful for dynamically referencing cells based on certain criteria.

Tips for Mastering Cell Referencing:

·~~Clarity is Key:~~ Use clear and descriptive cell names to enhance the readability and maintainability of your formulas, especially when using complex cell references.

·Error Checking: Excel aids you by highlighting potential errors in cell references. Pay close attention to these warnings and ensure your references are accurate.

·Explore Online Resources: The internet abounds with tutorials and resources on advanced cell referencing techniques. Don't hesitate to seek out additional learning materials as you expand your Excel expertise.

Cell references are the cornerstone of powerful formulas in Excel. By mastering relative and absolute references, combining them strategically, and exploring advanced techniques, you unlock the full potential of formula creation. Remember, practice and exploration are key to becoming a true cell referencing champion in Excel!

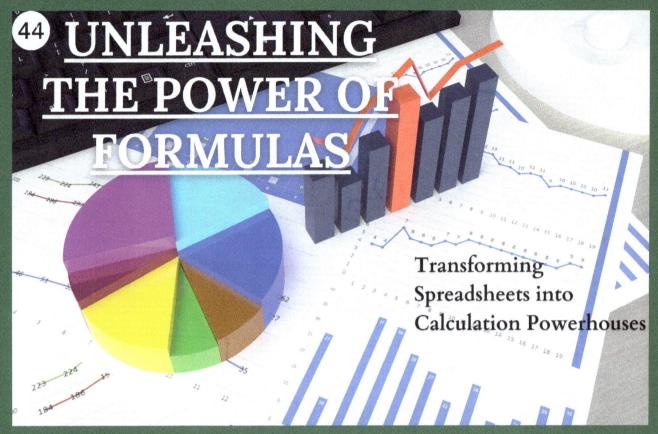

44 UNLEASHING THE POWER OF FORMULAS

Transforming Spreadsheets into Calculation Powerhouses

Welcome, spreadsheet enthusiasts! Numbers might seem daunting at first, but fear not! Excel empowers you to ditch the manual calculations and harness the magic of formulas. This chapter equips you with the knowledge to create formulas, automating calculations and transforming your spreadsheets into efficient tools for data analysis.

Understanding Formulas: Your Spreadsheet Superpower

Formulas are instructions you provide to Excel, dictating how it should manipulate data and perform calculations. They begin with an equal sign (=) followed by an expression that tells Excel what operations to execute. Formulas unlock a world of possibilities, allowing you to:

·**Automate Calculations:** Simplify repetitive calculations by setting up formulas that update automatically when the underlying data changes. This eliminates errors and saves you time.

·**Analyze Data:** Perform complex calculations and data analysis using built-in functions within formulas. You can uncover trends, identify patterns, and gain valuable insights from your data.

·**Create Dynamic Spreadsheets:** Formulas make your spreadsheets interactive. As you modify data, the formulas automatically recalculate, keeping your results up-to-date and reliable.

Building Your First Formula – A Step-by-Step Guide:

Let's embark on a journey to create your first formula!

1.	**Choose the Result Cell:** Click on the cell where you want the calculated outcome to be displayed.

2.	**Initiate with the Equal Sign (=):** This signifies the beginning of your formula.

3.	**Numbers or Cell References:** Enter the numerical values you want to use in your calculation directly within the formula (e.g., =5 + 3) or click on the cells containing the values you want to reference (e.g., =A1 + B2).

4. Operators (+, -, , /): Include mathematical operators to specify the type of calculation you want Excel to perform (addition, subtraction, multiplication, division).

5. Press Enter: Once you've constructed your formula, hit Enter. Excel will calculate the result based on your instructions and display it in the chosen cell.

Example: Calculating Total Sales

Imagine you have sales figures in cells B2, B3, and B4. To calculate the total sales and display it in cell B5, you can use the following formula:

Excel

=B2 + B3 + B4

In this formula, Excel adds the values in cells B2, B3, and B4 and displays the sum (total sales) in cell B5.

Formula Examples for Everyday Use:

Here are some additional formula examples you can experiment with:

·**Subtraction:** =C2 - B2 (Subtracts the value in cell B2 from the value in cell C2)

·**Multiplication:** =D3 5 (Multiplies the value in cell D3 by 5)

·**Division:** =E4 / 2 (Divides the value in cell E4 by 2)

Beyond the Basics: Exploring Built-in Functions

Excel offers a vast library of built-in functions that extend your formulaic capabilities. These functions perform specific calculations, data analysis tasks, and manipulations. Here are some commonly used functions to get you started:

·**SUM:** Calculates the sum of a range of cells (e.g., =SUM(A1:A10))

·**AVERAGE:** Calculates the average of a range of cells (e.g., =AVERAGE(B2:B8))

·**COUNT:** Counts the number of cells containing numerical values within a range (e.g., =COUNT(C1:C15))

·**COUNTIF:** Counts the number of cells within a range that meet a specific criterion (e.g., =COUNTIF(D2:D20, ">50")) – This formula counts the number of cells in D2:D20 that have values greater than 50.

Tips for Formula Success:

·**Start Simple:** Begin with basic formulas involving numbers and cell references. As you gain confidence, explore more complex functions and combinations.

·**Utilize the Formula Bar:** The formula bar displays your formula as you type and provides a live preview of the result. This helps you identify errors and visualize the calculation process.

·**Practice Makes Perfect:** Experiment with different formulas and functions. The more you practice, the more comfortable you'll become with building powerful formulas in Excel.

·**Seek Online Help:** The internet abounds with resources and tutorials on Excel formulas. Don't hesitate to consult online guides or communities for further learning.

Nesting Formulas for Complex Calculations:

Formulas can be nested within each other, allowing you to perform complex calculations in a single expression. Imagine you have product prices in cells B2, B3, and B4, and quantities in cells

C2, C3, and C4. You want to calculate the total cost for each product (price multiplied by quantity) and then add a 7.5% sales tax on the total cost. Here's how you can achieve this with nested formulas:

Excel

= (B2 C2) (1 + 0.075)

In this formula, the inner calculation (B2 C2) multiplies the price and quantity for each product. The result is then multiplied by (1 + 0.075), which calculates the total cost including a 7.5% sales tax.

Logical Functions for Conditional Calculations:

Excel offers a range of logical functions that enable you to perform calculations based on specific conditions. These functions evaluate whether a statement is true or false and return a corresponding value (usually 1 for TRUE and 0 for FALSE). Here's an example:

·IF Function: This function checks a condition and returns a specific value if the condition is true, and a different value if it's false. For instance, the formula =IF(A1>100, "High", "Low") would display "High" in the cell if the value in A1 is greater than 100, and "Low" otherwise.

Formula References: Leveraging Existing Calculations

You can leverage existing formulas within your new formulas to create a chain of calculations. This eliminates the need to repeat calculations and promotes dynamic updates throughout your spreadsheet. For example, imagine you have a formula in cell B5 that calculates the total sales (as discussed earlier). You can reference this formula (=B5) in another formula to perform further calculations based on the total sales figure.

Error Handling: Keeping Your Formulas Foolproof

Even the best formula builders encounter errors. Excel provides error handling functions that identify and manage errors within your formulas. These functions display informative messages or substitute alternative values when errors occur, ensuring the integrity of your calculations. A common error handling function is ISERROR, which checks if a formula has resulted in an error.

Tips for Mastering Advanced Formulas:

·Break Down Complex Formulas: If a formula seems overwhelming, break it down into smaller, more manageable steps. This can help you understand the logic behind each calculation within the nested formula.

·Utilize Online Resources: The internet offers a wealth of tutorials and examples on advanced formula construction. Explore these resources to discover new techniques and expand your formulaic repertoire.

·Experiment and Explore: Don't be afraid to experiment with different formulas and functions. The more you practice, the more comfortable you'll become with building robust and efficient formulas in Excel.

By mastering the art of formula creation, you unlock the true power of Excel. From performing complex calculations to conducting data analysis, formulas empower you to transform your spreadsheets into powerful tools for decision-making and problem-solving. Remember, consistent practice and exploration are key to becoming a formula whiz in Excel!

FUNCTION FRENZY! EXPLORING BUILT-IN FUNCTIONS FOR SPREADSHEET MASTERY

Welcome, spreadsheet adventurers! We've conquered the basics of formulas and delved into their power. Now, let's embark on a journey through the exciting realm of Excel functions! Functions are pre-built formulas that perform specific calculations, data analysis tasks, and manipulations. Mastering these functions elevates your spreadsheets from simple number crunchers to powerful tools for data exploration and insight generation. This chapter equips you with the knowledge to utilize common Excel functions, transforming you from a function fumbler into a spreadsheet whiz.

Understanding Excel Functions:

Imagine functions as your trusty tools in the spreadsheet workshop. Each function has a specific purpose, taking in certain inputs (arguments) and delivering a desired output based on those arguments. For example, the SUM function takes a range of cells as its argument and returns the total sum of the values within that range.

Benefits of Utilizing Functions:

·**Efficiency:** Functions save you time and effort. Instead of writing lengthy formulas from scratch, you can leverage pre-built functions to perform complex calculations with ease.

·**Accuracy:** Functions minimize the risk of errors, as they are pre-defined and thoroughly tested by Microsoft.

·**Consistency:** Functions ensure consistency in your calculations across your spreadsheet, especially when dealing with repetitive tasks.

Common Function Categories:

Excel offers a vast library of functions, categorized based on their functionalities. Here are some commonly used categories for beginners:

·**Math and Trigonometry Functions:** Perform basic and advanced mathematical calculations (SUM, AVERAGE, COUNT, POWER, SIN, COS, TAN).

·**Logical Functions:** Evaluate conditions and return results based on true or false statements (IF, AND, OR, NOT).

·**Lookup and Reference Functions:** Retrieve specific data from different parts of your spreadsheet (VLOOKUP, HLOOKUP, INDEX, MATCH).

·**Text Functions:** Manipulate text data within cells (CONCATENATE, LEFT, RIGHT, MID, UPPER, LOWER).

·**Date and Time Functions:** Perform calculations and manipulations on dates and times (TODAY, NOW, YEAR, MONTH, DAY).

Function Frenzy: Examples in Action!

Let's explore some common functions and see them in action:

1. **SUM Function:** Calculates the sum of values within a range of cells. Let's say you have sales figures in cells B2, B3, and B4. You can use the following formula to calculate the total sales:

Excel

=SUM(B2:B4)

2. **AVERAGE Function:** Calculates the average of values within a range of cells. Imagine you have exam scores in cells C1 to C5. You can use the following formula to calculate the average score:

Excel

=AVERAGE(C1:C5)

3. **IF Function:** Checks a condition and returns a specific value if the condition is true, and a different value if it's false. For instance, the formula =IF(A1>100, "High", "Low") would display "High" in the cell if the value in A1 is greater than 100, and "Low" otherwise.

Tips for Function Mastery:

·**Function Wizard:** Don't be afraid to utilize the Function Wizard (located on the Formulas tab). This interactive tool guides you through choosing the appropriate function, entering arguments, and understanding its purpose.

·**Explore Online Resources:** The internet abounds with tutorials and examples on various Excel functions. Don't hesitate to consult online resources to discover new functions and expand your repertoire.

·**Practice Makes Perfect:** Experiment with different functions in your spreadsheets. The more you practice, the more comfortable you'll become with selecting appropriate functions and applying them effectively.

Beyond the Basics: Exploring Advanced Functions

As you progress in your Excel journey, you'll discover a vast array of advanced functions for more complex tasks. Some examples include:

·**VLOOKUP and HLOOKUP:** These functions are powerhouses for retrieving specific data based on certain criteria within your spreadsheet.

·**COUNTIF and SUMIF:** These functions allow you to count or sum cells that meet specific conditions.

·**TEXT Functions:** These functions provide granular control over text manipulation, enabling you to format, extract, and modify text data within your spreadsheets.

Functions are the building blocks of powerful and versatile spreadsheets. By mastering common functions and exploring advanced options, you unlock the true potential of Excel. Remember, consistent practice and exploration are key to becoming a function fanatic in Excel!

CONQUERING SPREADSHEETS

Mastering Lookup, Conditional Counting, and Text Manipulation Functions

Welcome, spreadsheet superheroes! We've explored the fundamentals of formulas and delved into the world of charts. Now, it's time to refine your skills with some powerful functions that unlock advanced data manipulation within your spreadsheets. This chapter equips you with three sets of essential functions: **VLOOKUP and HLOOKUP** for efficient data retrieval, **COUNTIF and SUMIF** for conditional counting and summing, and **TEXT functions** for transforming and controlling text data within your spreadsheets.

Lookup Functions: Finding Your Data Fast

Imagine a massive library filled with information. Lookup functions act like librarians, helping you find specific data within your spreadsheets quickly and effortlessly. Here, we'll explore two commonly used lookup functions: VLOOKUP and HLOOKUP.

·VLOOKUP (Vertical Lookup): A champion at searching for data in tables organized in columns. It searches a specific column (lookup column) within the table and returns the value from a different column (return column) based on a match with a provided lookup value.

Example: VLOOKUP in Action

Let's say you have a table containing employee IDs, names, and department codes. You want to find the department code for a specific employee ID (lookup value). Here's a sample VLOOKUP formula to achieve this:

Excel

=VLOOKUP(A1, B2:E7, 3, FALSE)

·A1: This is the cell containing the employee ID you're looking up (lookup value).

·B2:E7: This is the table containing your employee data (range).

·3: This specifies the column index within the table (B2:E7) from which you want to retrieve the data (department code in this case). In our example, the department code is in the third column (counting from the leftmost column as 1).

·FALSE: This indicates an exact match is required.

HLOOKUP (Horizontal Lookup): Similar to VLOOKUP, but searches for data in tables organized in rows. It searches a specific row (lookup row) within the table and returns the value from a different column (return column) based on a match with a provided lookup value.

Using VLOOKUP and HLOOKUP Effectively:

·**Understand Your Data:** Ensure your data is organized in a clear table format with proper column and row headers for lookup functions to work effectively.

·**Choose the Right Function:** Select VLOOKUP for data in columns and HLOOKUP for data in rows.

Be Specific with Lookup Values: Provide accurate lookup values to ensure the functions retrieve the correct data.

·**Use Error Handling (Optional):** Consider incorporating error handling mechanisms (like the IFERROR function) to handle cases where the lookup value might not be found in the table.

Conditional Counting and Summing: Counting What Matters

·**COUNTIF:** A workhorse for counting cells that meet a specific criterion.

Example: Counting Customers by Age Group

Let's say you have a customer list with age data. You want to count the number of customers within a specific age range (e.g., 25-30 years old). Here's a COUNTIF formula to achieve this:

Excel

=COUNTIF(C2:C100, ">25") // Assuming ages are in cells C2:C100

This formula counts the number of cells in the range C2:C100 that contain values greater than 25.

·**SUMIF:** A powerful tool for summing values within a range that meet a specific condition.

Example: Summing Sales Figures by Region

Let's say you have a sales data table with figures and corresponding regions. You want to calculate the total sales for a specific region (e.g., "North"). Here's a SUMIF formula to achieve this:

Excel

=SUMIF(B2:B100, "North", A2:A100) // Assuming regions are in B2:B100 and sales figures are in A2:A100

This formula sums the values in the range A2:A100 (sales figures) for rows where the corresponding values in B2:B100 (regions) match "North".

Using COUNTIF and SUMIF Effectively:

·**Define Clear Criteria:** Precisely define the condition you want to use for counting or summing (e.g., specific values, comparisons, text matches).

·**Ensure Criteria Range Matches Data Range:** The range containing the criteria you're evaluating (e.g., cells containing ages or regions) should correspond with the data range you want to count or sum from.

Text Functions: Mastering Text Manipulation in Spreadsheets

Text functions empower you to control, modify, and extract specific information from text data within your spreadsheets. Here, we'll explore some commonly used text functions for beginners:

·**LEFT:** Extracts a specified number of characters from the left side of a text string.

Example: Extracting First Names

Let's say you have a list of full names in a single column. You want to extract just the first names. Here's a LEFT formula to achieve this:

Excel

=LEFT(A2, FIND(" ", A2, 1) - 1) // Assuming full names are in A2 and subsequent cells

This formula extracts characters from cell A2, starting from the leftmost position, up to (but not including) the space character. The FIND function locates the position of the first space within the name.

·RIGHT: Extracts a specified number of characters from the right side of a text string.

Example: Extracting File Extensions

Let's say you have a list of filenames with extensions (e.g., ".docx", ".xlsx"). You want to extract just the extensions. Here's a RIGHT formula to achieve this:

Excel

=RIGHT(A2, LEN(A2) - FIND(".",A2, LEN(A2)-1)) // Assuming filenames are in A2 and subsequent cells

This formula extracts characters from cell A2, starting from the position of the last period (".") identified by the FIND function, and includes all characters to the right (including the period).

·MID: Extracts a specific number of characters from a starting position within a text string.

Example: Extracting Middle Initials

Let's say you have a list of full names with middle initials. You want to extract just the middle initials. Here's a MID formula (assuming a consistent format with a space before and after the middle initial) to achieve this:

Excel

=MID(A2, FIND(" ", A2, FIND(" ", A2, 1) + 1) + 1, 1) // Assuming full names are in A2 and subsequent cells

This formula uses the FIND function twice to locate the positions of the two spaces within the name. It then extracts one character starting from the position after the second space.

·UPPER: Converts all characters in a text string to uppercase.

Example: Standardizing Case

Let's say you have a list of customer names with inconsistent capitalization. You want to convert all names to uppercase for consistency. Here's a UPPER formula to achieve this:

Excel

=UPPER(A2) // Assuming names are in A2 and subsequent cells

·LOWER: Converts all characters in a text string to lowercase.

Text Functions: Tips and Tricks

·Explore Additional Functions: Excel offers a variety of other text functions, such as CONCATENATE (combining text strings), LEN (finding the length of a text string), and REPLACE (replacing specific text within a string).

·Nesting Functions: You can combine text functions with other functions for more complex manipulations. For instance, you can use LEFT and RIGHT together to extract specific parts of a text string.

·Error Handling: Consider incorporating error handling mechanisms (like the IFERROR function) to handle cases where text data might not be formatted as expected.

By mastering **VLOOKUP, HLOOKUP, COUNTIF, SUMIF,** and text functions, you unlock a new level of control over your spreadsheet data. You can efficiently retrieve specific information, perform conditional calculations, and manipulate text data to suit your needs. Remember, consistent practice and exploration are key to becoming a spreadsheet wizard!

BUILDING ADVANCED FORMULAS

Nesting & Conditioning – Unlocking the Full Potential of Excel

Welcome back, spreadsheet explorers! We've ventured through the fundamentals of formulas and harnessed the power of built-in functions. Now, it's time to elevate your formulaic skills by exploring the art of nesting and conditioning. These techniques empower you to construct complex calculations and dynamic spreadsheets that adapt to your data.

Nesting Formulas: Calculations Within Calculations

Imagine a nesting doll – one doll fits inside another, and another inside that. Nesting formulas in Excel works similarly. You can embed a formula within another formula, allowing you to perform multiple calculations in a single expression. This unlocks a world of possibilities for complex calculations.

Example: Calculating Discounted Prices with Tax

Let's say you have product prices in cells B2, B3, and B4, and discount rates in cells C2, C3, and C4 (as percentages). You also have a fixed sales tax rate of 7.5% in cell D1. You want to calculate the final price for each product after applying the discount and then adding the sales tax. Here's how you can achieve this with nested formulas:

Excel

$$= (B2 (1 - C2/100)) (1 + 0.075)$$

In this formula:

·The inner calculation (B2(1 - C2/100)) calculates the discounted price by multiplying the original price (B2) with the discount percentage (C2) adjusted to a decimal (by dividing by 100 and subtracting it from 1).

·The outer calculation (1 + 0.075) multiplies the discounted price by the total sales factor (including the 7.5% tax) to arrive at the final price.

Conditional Formulas: Decisions Within Your Spreadsheet

Conditional formulas incorporate logic into your calculations, enabling your formulas to make decisions based on specific conditions. This unlocks a new level of automation and flexibility in your spreadsheets.

The IF Function: A Gateway to Conditional Formulas

The IF function is the cornerstone of conditional formulas. It evaluates a condition and returns a specific value if the condition is true, and a different value if it's false. Here's the basic structure:

Excel

=IF(condition, value_if_true, value_if_false)

Example: Assigning Grades Based on Scores

Let's say you have exam scores in cells B2, B3, and B4. You want to assign letter grades based on the following criteria:

·90 or above: A

·80 to 89: B

·70 to 79: C

·Below 70: F

Here's a formula using nested IF functions to achieve this:

Excel

=IF(B2>=90, "A", IF(B2>=80, "B", IF(B2>=70, "C", "F")))

This formula uses a series of nested IF statements to evaluate the score and assign the corresponding letter grade.

Tips for Mastering Nesting and Conditioning:

·**Start Simple:** Begin with basic nested formulas and conditional statements using the IF function. As you gain confidence, gradually introduce more complex logic and nested calculations.

·**Break Down Complex Formulas:** If a nested formula seems overwhelming, break it down into smaller, more manageable steps. This can help you understand the logic behind each calculation within the nested formula.

·**Utilize Online Resources:** The internet offers a wealth of tutorials and examples on advanced formula construction with nesting and conditioning. Explore these resources to discover new techniques and expand your formulaic repertoire.

·**Test Thoroughly:** As you build complex formulas with nesting and conditions, ensure you test them thoroughly with various data scenarios to ensure they produce the expected results.

By mastering nesting and conditioning, you unlock the true potential of Excel formulas. You can perform intricate calculations, automate decision-making within your spreadsheets, and create dynamic tools for data analysis. Remember, consistent practice, exploration, and a willingness to experiment are key to becoming a nesting and conditioning champion in Excel!

PRESENTING YOUR DATA VISUALLY WITH CHARTS

Transforming Numbers into Insights

Welcome, spreadsheet storytellers! Numbers are powerful, but sometimes, a chart speaks a thousand words. Excel empowers you to create visually compelling charts that transform raw data into clear and impactful insights. This chapter equips you with the knowledge to craft effective charts, making your spreadsheets come alive and resonate with your audience.

Understanding the Power of Charts:

Charts translate complex data sets into easily digestible visuals. They reveal patterns, trends, and relationships that might be hidden within rows and columns of numbers. By presenting data visually, you can:

·**Simplify Communication:** Charts communicate complex information in a clear and concise way, making it easier for your audience to grasp key takeaways.

·**Highlight Trends and Patterns:** Visualizations excel at revealing trends and patterns within your data that might go unnoticed in a table format.

·**Engage Your Audience:** Charts capture attention and make your data more engaging, fostering better understanding and retention of information.

Choosing the Right Chart Type:

Excel offers a wide variety of chart types, each suited to different data presentations. Here are some commonly used chart types for beginners:

·**Column Charts:** Ideal for comparing categories or showing trends over time. Columns represent data values, making them suitable for comparing sales figures, inventory levels, or survey results across categories.

Bar Charts: Similar to column charts, but bars are horizontal. They are useful for comparing values across categories when space is limited, or when you want to emphasize comparisons between categories.

·Line Charts: Best suited for showing trends over time. Lines connect data points, allowing viewers to easily visualize how a value changes over a period.

·Pie Charts: Represent proportions of a whole. Slices of the pie chart represent different categories, and their size corresponds to the percentage of the whole they represent.

Creating Your First Chart: A Step-by-Step Guide

Let's create a chart to showcase sales figures for different product categories (e.g., Clothing, Electronics, Furniture). Here's how:

1. Highlight Your Data: Select the range of cells containing your data, including category labels (in the first column) and sales figures (in the subsequent columns).

2. Insert Chart: Navigate to the "Insert" tab on the Excel ribbon. Click the "Recommended Charts" button or choose a specific chart type from the gallery (e.g., Column Chart for this example).

3. Explore Chart Options: Excel will generate a default chart based on your data. You can customize the chart by clicking on different chart elements (e.g., chart title, axis labels, data series). The "Chart Design" tab on the ribbon provides formatting options like color schemes, font styles, and layout choices.

4. Refine and Present: Experiment with different chart formats and layouts to achieve the desired visual impact. Once you're satisfied with your chart, you can insert it within your spreadsheet or export it as a separate image file for presentations.

Charting Tips for Beginners:

·Match Chart Type to Data: Choose a chart type that effectively represents the kind of data you have. For instance, use line charts for trends, column charts for comparisons, and pie charts for proportions.

·Clarity is Key: Ensure your chart is clear and easy to understand. Use concise labels, appropriate colors, and a clean layout to avoid overwhelming your audience.

·Highlight Key Insights: Use chart elements like data labels or callouts to emphasize important trends or patterns within your data.

·Practice Makes Perfect: The more charts you create, the more comfortable you'll become with choosing the right chart type and customizing it for optimal impact.

Beyond the Basics: Exploring Advanced Charting Techniques

As you progress in your Excel journey, you can delve into more advanced charting features:

·Combo Charts: Combine different chart types (e.g., columns and lines) within a single chart to showcase multiple data aspects.

·Chart Formatting: Utilize advanced formatting options to customize chart elements like grids, data markers, and error bars for a more professional look.

·Interactive Charts: Excel allows you to create interactive charts with features like data filtering and drill-down capabilities, enhancing user engagement with your data visualizations.

Charts are powerful tools for transforming your spreadsheets from data repositories into impactful communication tools. By mastering the art of chart creation, you can unlock the stories within your data and effectively engage your audience. Remember, consistent practice, exploration, and a focus on clarity will make you a charting champion in Excel!

CHOOSING THE RIGHT CHART TYPE FOR THE JOB

Making Your Data Shine

Selecting the perfect chart type for your data is crucial for effective communication in Excel. A well-chosen chart illuminates trends, comparisons, and relationships within your data, while a poor choice can leave your audience confused. This section equips you with the knowledge to confidently select the most appropriate chart type for your data analysis and presentation needs.

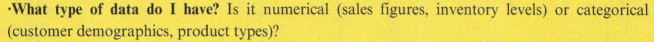

Understanding Your Data:

The first step is to thoroughly understand the kind of information you're trying to convey. Here are some key questions to consider:

·**What type of data do I have?** Is it numerical (sales figures, inventory levels) or categorical (customer demographics, product types)?

·**Am I comparing categories or showing trends over time?** These questions will guide you towards charts that excel at highlighting those specific relationships.

·**How many data series (sets of data) do I have?** Some charts, like pie charts, are best suited for a limited number of data series, while others, like line charts, can handle multiple series effectively.

Chart Types for Common Data Scenarios:

Here's a breakdown of popular chart types and when to use them:

·**Column Charts:** Shine for comparing categories. Columns rise vertically from the horizontal axis (x-axis), and their heights represent the values for each category. Use column charts to compare sales figures across product categories, website traffic by source, or customer satisfaction ratings.

·**Bar Charts:** Similar to column charts, but bars are horizontal. They excel at showcasing comparisons when space is limited or when you want to emphasize the differences in magnitude between categories. Use bar charts to compare budget allocations for different departments, customer demographics (age groups, income levels), or website traffic by device type (desktop, mobile, tablet).

·**Line Charts:** Champions at revealing trends over time. Lines connect data points plotted on the horizontal (time) and vertical (value) axes. Use line charts to show stock prices over time, website traffic trends by month, or project progress over weeks.

·**Pie Charts:** Represent proportions of a whole. Slices of the pie chart depict different categories, and their size corresponds to the percentage of the whole they represent. Use pie charts to showcase market share distribution among competitors, budget allocation by expense category, or customer satisfaction ratings (divided into "satisfied," "neutral," and "dissatisfied").

Choosing the Right Chart – A Decision Tree:

Here's a simplified decision tree to help you navigate chart selection:

1. Is your data numerical or categorical?

o **Numerical:** Proceed to step 2.

o **Categorical:** Consider column charts or bar charts for comparisons. Pie charts can work for proportions if you have a limited number of categories (ideally 4 or less).

2. Are you comparing categories or showing trends over time?

o **Comparing categories:** Column charts or bar charts are ideal choices.

o **Showing trends over time:** Line charts are your go-to option.

Additional Tips:

·**Combo Charts:** For showcasing multiple aspects of your data, consider combo charts. These combine different chart types (e.g., columns and lines) within a single visualization.

·**Chart Complexity:** While there are more advanced chart types available in Excel, it's often best to start with simpler options like those mentioned above. Complex charts can overwhelm your audience and obscure the core message.

·**Clarity and Conciseness:** Always prioritize clarity and conciseness in your chart design. Use clear labels, appropriate colors, and avoid excessive clutter. Let the data shine through!

By understanding your data and following these guidelines, you'll be well on your way to selecting the perfect chart type for every situation in Excel. Remember, the goal is to effectively communicate insights and tell a compelling story with your data.

SAVING YOUR WORKBOOKS

Safeguarding Your Spreadsheet Efforts

From meticulous data analysis to complex financial models, your workbooks deserve to be protected. This chapter equips you with the knowledge to master saving strategies, transforming you from a data loss apprentice into a spreadsheet preservation champion.

Understanding Saving:

Saving your workbook is akin to locking a treasure chest – it secures your valuable data and allows you to access it later. Excel offers various saving options, empowering you to choose the method that best suits your needs.

Saving Locally: Keeping Your Data Close

Saving locally means storing your workbook on your computer's hard drive or another local storage device (e.g., external hard drive). Here's a step-by-step guide to local saving:

1. Click the File Tab: Locate the "File" tab in the top left corner of your Excel window. This tab serves as your central hub for all file-related operations.

2. Save or Save As: You have two primary options:

   Save: If you've already saved your workbook with a chosen name and location, clicking "Save" simply updates the existing file with any recent changes.

   Save As: Use this option for the first time you save a workbook or if you want to create a copy of an existing workbook with a different name or location.

3. Choosing a Location: In the "Save As" window, navigate to the desired folder on your computer where you want to save your workbook. Utilize the folder hierarchy on the left side to navigate, or directly access commonly used locations (e.g., Documents, Desktop).

4. Naming Your Workbook: Provide a clear and descriptive name for your workbook in the "File name" box. Choose a name that reflects the content of your spreadsheet for easy identification later.

5. Saving the File: Click the "Save" button to finalize the local saving process. Your workbook will be stored on your chosen location on your computer.

Saving to the Cloud: Embracing Accessibility

Cloud storage services like OneDrive or Google Drive offer an alternative approach to saving your workbooks. Here's why cloud storage might be appealing:

1.   Accessibility: Access your workbooks from any device with an internet connection. This is ideal for working on the go or collaborating with others in real-time.

2.   Backup and Security: Cloud storage often provides automatic backups, safeguarding your data in case of local storage failure. Additionally, cloud services typically offer robust security measures to protect your files.

Saving to the Cloud: A Step-by-Step Guide

1. Click the File Tab: Navigate to the "File" tab as you would for local saving.

2. Save As: Choose the "Save As" option to specify a location and name for your workbook.

3. Cloud Storage Selection: Depending on your preferred cloud storage service (e.g., OneDrive, Google Drive), you might see a dedicated option within the "Save As" window. Click on that option to connect your Excel to your cloud storage account.

4. Location and Naming: Within your chosen cloud storage location, navigate to the desired folder and provide a clear name for your workbook.

5. Saving the File: Click "Save" to finalize the cloud saving process. Your workbook will be uploaded and stored securely in your cloud storage account.

Choosing the Right Saving Strategy:

The optimal saving strategy depends on your specific needs:

1.   Local Saving: Ideal if you primarily work on one computer and prefer offline access. It's also suitable for highly confidential workbooks you might not want stored in the cloud.

2.   Cloud Saving: Excellent for accessibility, collaboration, and automatic backups. However, internet connectivity is required to access your workbooks.

Tips for Effective Saving:

ü Develop a Saving Habit: Get into the routine of saving your workbook frequently, especially after making significant changes. Utilize the keyboard shortcut Ctrl + S for a quick save.

ü Utilize Versions: Many cloud storage services offer version history, allowing you to revert to previous versions of your workbook if needed.

ü Backup Regularly (Local Saving): Even with local saving, consider creating regular backups of your important workbooks on an external storage device for added security.

Your Data Guardian:

Mastering saving strategies empowers you to become a data guardian. By implementing effective saving habits and choosing the best approach for your needs, you'll ensure your valuable spreadsheet creations are safe, secure, and readily accessible. Remember, saving your work consistently is the cornerstone of safeguarding your efforts in Excel!

SHARE YOUR GENIUS!

Collaboration Made Easy in Excel

Welcome back, spreadsheet collaborators! The beauty of Excel lies not only in its analytical prowess but also in its ability to foster teamwork. This chapter equips you with the knowledge to share your workbooks with others, transforming you from a solitary spreadsheet surgeon into a collaborative maestro.

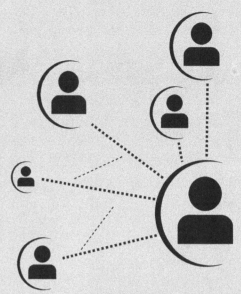

Understanding Workbook Sharing:

Sharing your workbook allows others to view, edit, or even comment on your spreadsheet. This functionality is instrumental for tasks like:

Ø **Teamwork:** Collaborate with colleagues on projects, brainstorm ideas, and work on the same spreadsheet simultaneously.

Ø **Feedback and Reviews:** Share your work with managers or clients to gather feedback and incorporate their suggestions directly into the workbook.

Ø **Distributing Information:** Disseminate reports or data summaries to wider audiences without needing to send individual copies.

Sharing Options in Excel:

Excel offers multiple ways to share your workbooks, catering to different needs and preferences:

Ø **Local File Sharing:** Share your workbook as a local file via email or file transfer services. However, this method doesn't facilitate real-time collaboration, and recipients might need compatible software to open the file.

Ø **Shared Workbooks (Legacy Feature):** This traditional method allows multiple users to edit a workbook stored on a shared network drive. However, it requires careful coordination to avoid conflicts when multiple users try to edit the same cells simultaneously.

Ø **Cloud-Based Collaboration:** Leveraging cloud storage services like OneDrive or Google Drive streamlines collaboration. Upload your workbook to the cloud, and invite others to view or edit it in real-time. This approach offers greater accessibility and eliminates the risk of file corruption due to conflicting edits.

Sharing Your Workbook via OneDrive (Step-by-Step Guide):

OneDrive serves as a popular cloud storage option for seamless collaboration in Excel. Here's a step-by-step guide to share your workbook using OneDrive:

1. **Save Your Workbook to OneDrive:** Begin by ensuring your workbook is saved to your OneDrive account. Click the "File" tab, then "Save As." Choose "OneDrive" from the available locations and navigate to the desired folder within your OneDrive storage. Click "Save" to upload the workbook to the cloud.

2. Share Permissions: Right-click on the uploaded workbook in your OneDrive online storage (accessed through a web browser) or within the OneDrive folder on your computer. Select "Share" from the context menu.

3. Inviting Collaborators: In the "Share" pane, enter the email addresses of the people you want to share the workbook with. Specify their access level:

Can edit: Allows collaborators to make changes to the workbook.

Can view: Grants view-only access, where users can see the workbook but cannot modify it.

4. Adding a Message (Optional): Include a brief message in the "Add a message (optional)" section to provide context or instructions for your collaborators.

5. Sending the Invite: Click the "Send" button to send invitations to your chosen collaborators. They will receive an email notification with a link to access the shared workbook.

Real–Time Collaboration and Conflict Resolution:

With cloud-based collaboration, multiple users can work on the same workbook simultaneously. Excel employs optimistic locking, allowing edits to proceed without interruption. However, occasional conflicts might arise if two users attempt to modify the same cell concurrently. In such cases, Excel highlights the conflicting changes, and users can choose which edit to retain.

Tips for Effective Collaboration:

Ø **Clear Communication:** Communicate clearly with your collaborators regarding roles, access levels, and editing protocols to avoid confusion and maintain a smooth workflow.

Ø **Version Control:** Cloud storage services often provide version history, allowing you to revert to previous versions of the workbook if necessary.

Ø **Utilize Comments:** The "Comments" feature allows collaborators to leave notes or questions directly within the spreadsheet, facilitating communication and feedback.

By mastering the art of sharing your workbooks, you transform from a solitary spreadsheet surgeon into a collaboration champion. Leverage the power of cloud-based collaboration to work effectively with others, share your expertise, and achieve your goals together. Remember, effective communication and clear expectations are key ingredients for successful spreadsheet collaboration!

50+ EXCEL FORMULAR

1. Math and Trigonometry Functions:

·SUM: Calculates the sum of values in a range (e.g., =SUM(A1:A10)).

·AVERAGE: Calculates the average of values in a range (e.g., =AVERAGE(B2:B15)).

·COUNT: Counts the number of cells containing numerical values (e.g., =COUNT(C2:C20)).

·COUNTIF: Counts cells meeting a specific criterion (e.g., =COUNTIF(D2:D10, ">50")).

·MIN: Returns the smallest value in a range (e.g., =MIN(E2:E8)).

·MAX: Returns the largest value in a range (e.g., =MAX(F3:F12)).

·ROUND: Rounds a number to a specified number of decimal places (e.g., =ROUND(G4, 2)).

·SQRT: Calculates the square root of a number (e.g., =SQRT(H5)).

·SIN: Calculates the sine of an angle (e.g., =SIN(I6)).

·COS: Calculates the cosine of an angle (e.g., =COS(J7)).

·TAN: Calculates the tangent of an angle (e.g., =TAN(K8)).

2. Logical Functions:

·IF: Performs a conditional test and returns a value based on the result (e.g., =IF(A1>100, "High", "Low")).

·AND: Returns TRUE if all conditions are true (e.g., =AND(B2>5, C2<15)).

·OR: Returns TRUE if any condition is true (e.g., =OR(D3="Yes", E3="No")).

·NOT: Reverses the logical outcome (e.g., =NOT(F4>0)).

3. Text Functions:

·LEFT: Extracts a specific number of characters from the left side of a text string (e.g., =LEFT(G5, 3)).

·RIGHT: Extracts a specific number of characters from the right side of a text string (e.g., =RIGHT(H6, 4)).

·MID: Extracts a specific number of characters from a starting position within a text string (e.g., =MID(I7, 8, 2)).

·UPPER: Converts all characters in a text string to uppercase (e.g., =UPPER(J8)).

·LOWER: Converts all characters in a text string to lowercase (e.g., =LOWER(K9)).

·CONCATENATE: Combines multiple text strings into a single string (e.g., =CONCATENATE(A1, " ", B1)).

·LEN: Finds the length of a text string (e.g., =LEN(C2)).

·FIND: Locates the position of a specific text string within another string (e.g., =FIND("Sales", D3)).

4. Date and Time Functions:

·TODAY: Returns the current date (e.g., =TODAY()).

·NOW: Returns the current date and time (e.g., =NOW()).

·DATE: Converts a year, month, and day into a serial date number (e.g., =DATE(2024, 3, 25)).

·YEAR: Extracts the year from a date (e.g., =YEAR(A1)).

·MONTH: Extracts the month from a date (e.g., =MONTH(B2)).

·DAY: Extracts the day from a date (e.g., =DAY(C3)).

5. Lookup and Reference Functions:

·VLOOKUP: Searches for data in a table organized in columns and returns a value from a different column based on a match with a provided lookup value (e.g., =VLOOKUP(D4, E2:H10, 3, FALSE)).

·HLOOKUP: Searches for data in a table organized in rows and returns a value from a different column based on a match with a provided lookup value (e.g., =HLOOKUP(A5, B2:F7, 2, FALSE)).

6. Statistical Functions:

·COUNTBLANK: Counts the number of blank cells within a range (e.g., =COUNTBLANK(A1:A10)).

·COUNTIF: Counts cells meeting a specific criterion (covered earlier).

·SUMIF: Sums values in a range that meet a specific criterion (e.g., =SUMIF(B2:B15, ">10", C2:C15)).

·AVERAGEIF: Calculates the average of values in a range that meet a specific criterion (e.g., =AVERAGEIF(C2:C20, "East", D2:D20)).

·VAR: Calculates the variance of a population (e.g., =VAR(D3:D12)).

·STDEV: Calculates the standard deviation of a population (e.g., =STDEV(E4:E18)).

7. Financial Functions:

·PMT: Calculates the periodic payment for a loan (e.g., =PMT(10%, 36, 100000)).

·FV: Calculates the future value of an investment (e.g., =FV(5%, 20, -200, 10000)).

·IRR: Calculates the internal rate of return for a series of cash flows (e.g., =IRR(B2:B12)).

·NPV: Calculates the net present value of an investment (e.g., =NPV(10%, B2:B12)).

8. Database Functions:

·SUMIFS: Similar to SUMIF, but allows you to specify multiple criteria (e.g., =SUMIFS(A2:A10, B2:B10, ">50", C2:C10, "North")).

·COUNTIFS: Similar to COUNTIF, but allows you to specify multiple criteria (e.g., =COUNTIFS(A2:A10, ">50", B2:B10, "North")).

·AVERAGEIFS: Similar to AVERAGEIF, but allows you to specify multiple criteria (e.g., =AVERAGEIFS(C2:C10, A2:A10, ">50", B2:B10, "North")).

9. Text to Columns and Columns to Text Functions:

·TEXTSPLIT: Splits text into multiple columns based on a delimiter (e.g., =TEXTSPLIT(A1, ",", TRUE)).

·TEXTJOIN: Joins multiple text strings into a single string using a delimiter (e.g., =TEXTJOIN(",", TRUE, A2:A5)).

·TRANSPOSE: Transposes rows and columns of a range (e.g., =TRANSPOSE(B2:E5)).

10. Logical Functions (Advanced):

·XOR: Returns TRUE if a different number of conditions are TRUE compared to FALSE (e.g., =XOR(A1>0, B1<5)).

·SWITCH: Evaluates multiple expressions and returns a value based on the first true match (e.g., =SWITCH(C1, "Apple", "Fruit", "Orange", "Citrus", TRUE)).

Remember: This list provides a glimpse into the vast world of Excel formulas. Explore online resources and experiment with different formulas to expand your spreadsheet mastery!

My Note

My Note

My Note

My Note

My Note